Red Silk

Red Silk

An Anthology of
South Asian Canadian Women Poets

EDS. RISHMA DUNLOP & PRISCILA UPPAL

For Shenee,

Hope you enjoy.

Yours, Priscila Uppal

2005

Mansfield Press

Library and Archives Canada Cataloguing in Publication

Red silk: an anthology of South Asian Canadian women poets / editors, Rishma Dunlop,
Priscila Uppal; authors, Hiro Boga ... [et al.].

ISBN 1-894469-16-X

1. Canadian poetry (English)—Women authors. 2. Canadian poetry (English)—South
Asian Canadian authors. 3. Canadian poetry (English)—21st century. I. Dunlop, Rishma,
II. Uppal, Priscila III. Boga, Hiro IV. Title.

PS8283.A8R43 2004   C811'.60809287   C2004-906310-3

Cover Design: Meera Sethi
Interior Design: Marijke Friesen

The publication of *Red Silk*
has been generously supported by
The Canada Council for the Arts and
The Ontario Arts Council.

The editors would like to thank our publisher, Denis De Klerck and Mansfield Press; our
editorial assistant Kulsoom Anwer; Kuldip Gill; and York University programs and
colleagues for their continued support.

Mansfield Press Inc.
25 Mansfield Avenue, Toronto, Ontario, Canada. M6J 2A9
Publisher: Denis De Klerck
www.mansfieldpress.net

TABLE OF CONTENTS

Travelers, Like Us: An Introduction to *Red Silk*

Like most anthology projects, the impetus behind *Red Silk* derived from a mix of professional and personal concerns. While anthologies of South Asian Canadian writing are not completely absent from Canadian literature, only a handful have been published over the last two decades, few dedicated to publishing poetry, and even fewer introducing women poets. However, without these pioneering anthologies, a project like ours could not have been attempted, let alone achieved. As Diane McGifford and Judith Kearns point out in *Shakti's Words: An Anthology of South Asian Canadian Poetry* (TSAR publications, 1990), "Until the 1960s there were no works in English by South Asians"(ix). More than four decades later, while South Asian Canadian fiction has received national and international status and acclaim, the poetry has remained in its shadow, and South Asian Canadian women writers have received much less attention than their male counterparts.

Ours is not a new complaint. When Suwanda Sugunasiri edited *The Whistling Thorn: South Asian Canadian Fiction* (Mosaic Press, 1994), the introduction included the following caveat: "if there are only three women writers here (Lakshmi Gill, Surjeet Kalsey, Uma Parameswaran), it is not unreflective of the larger reality of the South Asian Canadian scene"(intro); and in *The Geography of Voice* (TSAR publications, 1992), Diane McGifford adds, "Generally South Asian Canadian women have written more poetry and the men more prose"(xv), and it is likely that the lack of critical attention and commercial success lamented by nearly all Canadian poets also adds to the perception of an absence of South Asian Canadian women poets, especially the new and emerging voices of the new millennium. The 1990s anthologies of *The Geography of Voice* and *Shakti's Words* highlight the work of South Asian Canadian women poets Lakshmi Gill, Himani Bannerji, and Uma Parameswaran, and certainly Arun Mukherjee is correct in perceiving a publication of South Asian women's writing in English "a pioneering event"(*Her Mother's Ashes*, ix), but these names, while they have earned their due in these publications, are not exclusively representative of the range and diversity of writing by South Asian Canadian women poets today.

These critical concerns were brought to consciousness for our editors in tandem with several other academic and creative explorations. Both in her academic and creative work, Rishma Dunlop, who had the initial idea for *Red Silk*, had been exploring South Asian literature, immigrant and diasporic identities and their relationships to memory, history, class and gender. Delving deeper and more specifically into South Asian Canadian writing, and reading the existing anthologies, new questions of theoretical, cultural, and aesthetic interest rose to the forefront. Where were the new and emergent poetic voices? Mixed race voices? Hybrid identity? The voices of those born and raised in Canada? How were these women poets writing about their lives, tackling issues of national and cultural identity? Issues of class and gender?

With these questions in mind, and upon hearing that poet and colleague Priscila Uppal was of mixed race identity which included a South Asian background, Rishma Dunlop decided to approach Uppal with the idea of compiling an anthology that would highlight the new wave of poetry being written by South Asian Canadian women. Although Uppal had resisted identification as a "South Asian" poet or academic, her work frequently explored issues of gender, ethnicity, and nationalism. She had also read extensively in the area of South Asian Canadian literature.

Dunlop then approached Denis De Klerck, publisher of Mansfield Press, who is committed to bringing new, diverse voices to his press and to the Canadian poetry scene, and he agreed to publish the proposed anthology if both writers were willing to undertake the anthology as editors, and also as contributing poets. The proposal led the editors to consider, first and foremost, whether it was actually a fruitful exercise to group together what one hoped would be a diverse and eclectic mix of writers under the heading "South Asian Canadian women"?

Our title *Red Silk* provokes deeply embedded connotations for women of South Asian heritage, as historically and culturally red is the color of happiness and joyful celebration. Red silk saris, *salvar kameez,* and other traditional attire embroidered with gold brocade are worn by traditional brides across the Indian sub-continent and these historical and cultural traditions are maintained by many South Asians in Canada and in the world. From this fabric, symbolic and real, myriad connotations and provocations emerge for contemporary South Asian Canadian women poets. These points of departure include considerations of exoticism, eroticism, the paradoxes and contradictions between feminist concerns, women's traditional roles, submission, oppression, hybrid and diasporic identities and the material lives of modern women. Red silk as symbolic of traditional feminine roles for South Asians, invites questions and challenges to accepted notions of South Asian identities, women's identities, and opens the door to re-imagine, re-write or re-invent these roles and symbols.

Were we convinced, as editor Nurjehan Aziz was, in collecting together short stories by South Asian Canadian and American women in *Her Mother's Ashes* (TSAR 1994), and then again in Her *Mother's Ashes: II* (TSAR 1998), that "South Asian women despite all their differences possess enough in common to make the enterprise of collecting their works in a single volume a meaningful one"(vii)? We realized quickly as submissions came in, that there could be no homogenizing tendencies as has been the custom of Western scholarship; the category of "South Asian woman" is a reductive, constrictive and false categorization and is used here in full knowledge of the inadequacy of any such label.

As Arun Mukherjee points out, the term "South Asian" is inadequate to express our diversities. The terms South Asian and East Indian include vast linguistic, ethnic and religious differences as well as the historical legacies of markers of class and caste identities. South Asians with origins in the Indian sub-continent include those who are Punjabi, Bengali, Marathi, Tamil, Telegu, Malayali, Parsi, Sikh, Hindu, Muslim, Christian, to name only a few possibilities (Mukherjee, p.x).

Our own backgrounds reflect the vast differences between those who might be categorized as South Asian Canadian women. Rishma Dunlop was born in India, the daughter of Sikh parents, a biochemist and a teacher, and immigrated to Canada in 1958 when Dunlop was a small child. She grew up in Beaconsfield, Quebec. Priscila Uppal was born in 1974 in Ottawa and grew up with an absent Brazilian mother and a quadriplegic father of South Asian origin. Neither Dunlop nor Uppal were specifically instructed in the religion, language, or traditions of South Asian culture, although these traditions would have been present in peripheral ways. Uppal had written a novel about Catholic nuns, a collection of poetry responding to the post-September 11th reality through the lens of Greek mythology, among others. Dunlop had written essays, a radio play and a PhD dissertation which explored ancestral roots in India, and had published collections of poetry deeply connected to women's bodies and desire. We realized that our own work and background were vastly different. We felt that given a larger body of work by South Asian Canadian women poets, we would have a much better idea of what poetry was actually being written, and then we would have a better basis for significant comparison. In fact we wanted the anthology to reflect a range of difference to bear out our conviction that there is no monolithic South Asian culture.

We were keenly interested in reading what other women were writing about, not to the exclusion of South Asian Canadian male poetry, but because we were aware, as earlier editors were, of more poetry by South Asian Canadian women than by South Asian Canadian men, and our own creative and academic work was also heavily invested in Barbara Godard's formulation, that "the impact of feminist scholarship has been to show that gender is a fundamental organizing category of human experience and the creation of knowledge"(1). And yet, we knew too, by our own research and creative work, that it would be difficult to even attempt to predict in what ways these women would respond to the roles of women in their work.

In deciding what "South Asian Canadian Woman Poet" actually meant, we sought guidance from the predecessors to *Red Silk*. *Shakti's Words: An Anthology of South-Asian Canadian Women's Poetry* edited by Diane McGifford and Judith Kearns (TSAR publications, 1990) provided us with a workable definition of writers rooted in the Indian sub-continent: "the writing of South Asian Canadian women who traced their origins from one of the following South-Asian countries: India, Sri Lanka, Pakistan, and Bangladesh . . . directly to

Canada from one of the South Asian countries or indirectly by way of Britain, or British Colonies, such as those from Eastern and Southern Africa, the Caribbean, and the Pacific Islands"(ix). We specified in our call for submissions that we were looking for ten to fifteen pages of poetry as yet unpublished in book form, and while this was a South Asian Canadian women's poetry anthology, we welcomed poetry on any theme. In fact, our request was: "we want to see the work you are actually writing," in the hope of receiving a more accurate sample of the poetic concerns and vastness of experience of our poets rather than only poetry about being South Asian.

Right from the beginning the editors and publisher had agreed upon a portfolio-style anthology so that poets could be introduced not by one or two pieces but by a body of work which would more adequately convey their poetic interests and sensibilities. Our selection process was based first on our own discernment of literary merit. In addition, we also selected with variety of form and range of voice in mind. Luckily, these two notions are certainly not mutually exclusive and we feel that every contributor to *Red Silk* demonstrates high literary merit as well as originality in terms of poetic approach or formal experimentation. While we did receive a lot of poetry which can be identified as exploring the South Asian experience in particular, we also received love poems, sound poetry, poems about sexual awakening, poetry without any reference to South Asian origins. We asked for a "Poet's Statement" from each contributor, a paragraph introducing each writer's poetic concerns, philosophical frameworks, or any other information about her artistic practice which she cared to highlight for the reader to introduce her poems.

What did we find? Our poets are formally diverse. Herein are prose poems, sonnets, ghazals, sound poetry, lyric fragments, sequences, and long poems. The proliferation of long poems and sequences was, at first, surprising; however, the complexity of experience and expression evident in the poets' explorations seems to necessitate the longer verse forms. In addition, over the last few decades, the long poem form has frequently been cited as a dominant Canadian form, with several critics concurring with D.M.R. Bentley that the form "may have begun on the margins but now holds the center"(18), and with Frank M. Tierney and Angela Robbeson distinguishing further that it might be "distinctively Canadian in its documentary aspects, often serving a topographical and memorial function"(1). The long poem and poetic sequence offerings in *Red Silk* ought to be fruitfully considered as belonging to that tradition.

While the traditional red silk wedding sari is mentioned in several poems, red silk, for its editors and its writers, can also be interpreted as a locus for the exploration of notions of tradition, transplantation, stereotype, oppression, submission, womanhood, motherhood, that all of our poets in some way explore. As editors, we were both pleased and surprised to find a number of common threads among our writers, while each writer has also retained individual aesthetic and theoretical strategies for examining these themes. Many of the poems deal with the tensions between how history is taught and how it is remembered, but also how it is invented and reinvented. Memory plays a crucial structuring role for the transmission of family histories between generations, but also between forms.

Mothers appear everywhere in these pages. Perhaps this is a reflection of writing by women as a whole, the need to both identify with and rebel against one's first and most significant image of woman and mother. However, we'd like to suggest further that the proliferation of mothers might also be under-stood as concurrent with the investigation of history and memory evident in the poems. How the women remember their mothers says a great deal about how they envision the world and their own place in it.

Travel has ended up being the dominant theme of the collection. Each of these poets isolate travel to and from places. Whether real or imagined, historical or memory-based, the prime energy of the poetic lines is movement, and place is as fluid in the work as language itself. The convergence and blurring of linguistic identities is also evident; herein are Punjabi words, French, Latin, cultural slang. The hybridized tongues reflect the multiple languages and linguistic traditions from which these poets draw their subject matter and semiotic language bases.

We did not find an essentialized South Asian Canadian national or cultural identity, nor did we find one unifying experience of gender among these poets. What is most common between all of us might be what is most common between all writers: the imagination is more crucial to notions of selfhood and family and home than categories of gender, actual national boundaries, home-lands, and ancestral roots, because through the imagination we can travel the greatest distances and claim so much as our own.

While previous anthologies of South Asian Canadian writing have sought to expose a "distinctiveness of the 'in-Canada' South Asian immigrant experience, a distinctiveness that leaves most of us wincing and ashamed. . . . [an] icy, hostile social environment where they feel themselves doubly marginalized: first because they are immigrants and second because they belong to racial, often linguistic, and usually religious minorities"(Geography of Voice, viii), our anthology proves that this experience need not be the only one. Many of our writers were born in Canada, or were brought to Canada at very young ages. Many of our writers are mixed race. In fact, our three youngest contributors belong to both categories. In the end, these eleven writers are firmly Canadian writers. Hybridity is not something to be grieved, but something to be celebrated. They are not struggling with the same anger or racial oppression of their predecessors, but are claiming their experiences without guilt and without apology. Who we are is not something to be discovered in our genetics or in the history books; it is to be discovered in the many forms of the imagination.

However, while these writers can be legitimately perceived as engaged in several common practices and theoretical explorations, they are also individual poets in their own right, and we would like to take the time and opportunity here to say a few words about each poet, to offer up our thoughts and reactions as editors to the poetry we have chosen to highlight in *Red Silk*.

Hiro Boga's selection of connected lyric fragments reads as a series of contradictions, of conflicting and opposing emotions and drives. The domestic world and the mythical world combine as Hindu mythology rubs up against the Sears catalogue for the poet's attention. "Every no bears in its belly the sibilant/yes," Boga writes, and the poem moves less like a spiritual conversion than a mix of protest and celebration, stops and starts, as the mythic and the mundane compete for the same space.

Rishma Dunlop's individual lyrics also explore competing and sometimes conflicting spaces of identity as the apprenticeship of the student, the artist, the lover, and the poet are carried out in memory, in the world of books, in the post-colonial experience of her childhood, and the urban cityscape of her adulthood. Travel in her poems appears as a vehicle for memory and as a form of creation. "There is tenderness in every geography," she writes, while the geography of language is explored as another form of tenderness which ought not to be ignored.

From Kuldip Gill's selection we take the title of our introduction. In the poem "Four O'Clock Tea at Harrison Hot Springs Hotel" Gill juxtaposes the colonial experience in India with post-colonial life in British Columbia, elegantly remaking Delhi on the west coast. Her ability to combine cultures and experiences into a cohesive whole is also evident in her formal concerns. Persian forms such as the ghazal exist alongside the sonnet and the glosa.

Sonnet L'Abbé's selection is, arguably, the most edgy, even in-your-face. L'Abbé is not afraid to take risks, experiment, and diverge from previous work as she tackles post-colonial issues head-on in "Theory, My Natural Brown Ass," and international relations in "My Osama Bin Laden T-Shirt." Most intriguing about her work is the sense of play which permeates each poem as she invents herself, her language, and her ancestry: "Killarnoe, I decide, is the land/of our ancient people."

Danielle Lagah's selection is another long poem sequence which is as much detective work as it is poetry. The family history is told by various players (the poems are formatted like a play), and both writer and reader simultaneously piece together the story fragments about a girl poisoned to death under mysterious circumstances. Lagah's language is highly evocative and provocative, where the brutal reality of immigrant wives is set against other images of mundane domesticity. The exoticization and romanticization of India, the lush imagery and sensuality, continually shocks alongside grit, poverty, and disease.

Soraya Peerbaye's poetry is primarily sensory. Reading her work is like confronting both sides of a negative at once: "as I try to photograph/the light, the light photographs me." The rabbit image as one of girlhood adolescence bordering on womanhood expresses all the trappings of domesticity and femininity while intimating the power of sexuality and the larger public world. The vulnerability of the voice here is its strength and the poet risks the safe places for those with untapped potential.

Sharanpal Ruprai displays the most overt use of religious symbology in her poetic sequence. The reader enters a conflicted household, and one which you rarely see represented in Canadian poetry. The poems raise important questions about the roles of men and women, boys and girls, and how these roles get played out in the many rituals associated with one's faith and culture, and transplanted into another country. "I wonder how it must feel to carry/this weight," Ruprai writes. Her poetry is courageous, spanning the emotional gauntlet from shame to determination to humour.

Sandeep Sanghera's selection is populated by women. Family history, village history, colonial history, international history; all intersect in her poetry as the roles her female figures assume in diverse landscapes are examined. The poet is witness to all the comings and goings, the secrets and betrayals: "The women in this village/are the running off kind." The individual lyrics accumulate into a pledge of loyalty, not necessarily to a specific people or place, but to the transmission of stories in a community: "still a village will bear the weight of my tale/and the weight of your disbelief."

Shauna Singh Baldwin blends humor with seriousness as she makes use of bakeries, personal ads, holidays, and Hallmark cards in her poetry. This world is at once her world, where she has a stake in the political events of the present and the past, but one which also does not seem to take into account the needs and wants of its citizens. Questions of faith mix with moments of wonder as the poet seeks guidance in a time marked by violence and hypocritical gurus.

Proma Tagore's poetry also bears witness to the violence and marginalization of voice around her, at the same time that it celebrates difference and the sensuality of experience. From an elegy for Reena Virk in Victoria B.C., "November 14th," to lesbian love poems, to poems that respond to other writers, Tagore's poems are as diverse as they are dense. "I can hear the etchings of new maps," she writes, siding with the possible rather than the restrictive.

Priscila Uppal's long poem sequence does not so much describe the loss of a particular mother (no description of the woman is given at all) as it explores the nature of invention as a consolation for grief. Another detective story, the daughter refuses to be "tricked" by memory, and invents her own physical evidence, her mother's character, and her own familial identity, even to the point of imagining siblings. Everything must be created because so much has been destroyed. Her travels to hunt down her runaway mother occur not by the aid of memory, but through the imagination, "the last place she knows you will look."

No anthology can claim complete representation with equal balance served to all geographic regions, poetic traditions and affiliations, as well as to the diversity of cultural and religious traditions and sexual orientations a modern multicultural nation offers. We know there are multiple religious, cultural, and linguistic backgrounds within South Asian communities which are not represented here. We have a high Sikh Punjabi religious, linguistic, and cultural content. Many of our contributors live in Ontario and on the West Coast; however, this is most likely related to history and immigration patterns as these two regions have the highest populations of Canadians of South Asian descent. In addition, in response to our call for submissions for the anthology, we discovered some burgeoning movements, evidence of work-in-progress, though still at a developmental stage, of accomplishment in areas not traditionally associated with immigrant poetry, such as concrete poetry, and we think that if another anthology were undertaken in ten year's time, we would very likely find this work may have more representation from South Asian women writers.

Since we are all travelers, poetry is a source that can and does speak powerfully across differences; poetry is a language of many tongues, many geographies. There is a plethora of South Asian Canadian women's writing, and specifically women's poetry, being written. The works included here are not exercises in nostalgia; rather, they are imaginings and re-imaginings of history, memory, the material reality of lives, testifying to the fact that boundaries of nation, culture and gender are slippery inventions requiring continuous interrogation.

Rishma Dunlop and Priscila Uppal
Toronto 2004

Works Cited

Aziz, Nurjehan, ed. *Her Mother's Ashes.* Toronto: TSAR publications, 1994.

Aziz, Nurjehan, ed. *Her Mother's Ashes: II.* Toronto: TSAR publications, 1998.

Bentley, D.M.R. "Colonizing Canada: An Introductory Survey of the Canadian Long Poem." *Bolder Flights: Essays on the Canadian Long Poem.* Eds. Frank M. Tierney and Angela Robbeson. Ottawa: University of Ottawa Press, 1998. 151-159.

Godard, Barbara. *Gynocritics/gynocritics: Feminist Approaches to Canadian and Quebec Women Writers.* Toronto: ECW Press, 1987.

McGifford, Diane, ed. *The Geography of Voice.* Toronto: TSAR publications, 1992.

McGifford, Diane & Judith Kearns, eds. *Shakti's Words: An Anthology of South Asian Canadian Women's Poetry.* Toronto: TSAR publications, 1990.

Mukherjee, Arun. "Introduction." *Her Mother's Ashes.* Toronto: TSAR publications, 1994.

Rafiq, Fauzia, ed. *Aurat Durbar: The Court of Women, Writings By Women of South Asian Origin.* Toronto: Second Story Press, 1995.

Sugunasiri, Suwanda, ed. *The Whistling Thorn: South Asian Canadian Fiction.* Oakville: Mosaic Press, 1994.

Tierney, Frank M. & Angela Robbeson, eds. *Bolder Flights: Essays on the Canadian Long Poem.* Ottawa: University of Ottawa Press, 1998.

HIRO BOGA

Poetry articulates the archeology of my being; it gives resonance to all the layers of my experience, which without it remain separate and discrete. The roots of my poems are buried deep in my earliest sensory memories, and part way through a poem the cadences of language imprinted on my ear when I was growing up in Bombay emerge and all of a sudden it's a rainy night in monsoon season and I'm listening to the call of the pujari reciting from the Ramayana, and the chorus of voices chanting the response and the hiss of rain falling blends with this west coast silence embracing all my worlds in a profoundly musical wholeness.

Sarva Mangalam: Left Hand Poems

Mouth clamped shut, corners crimped tight
over teeth pressed against the soft insides.

Nothing will enter, nothing leave, this cave.

I am empty and intend to stay that way;
all my fire used up to digest what's already

been swallowed. If I don't die of it, I'll
live forever on the contents of my stomach

Now this is what I feed myself: sleep
in the nest of my feather bed; buttered
cream of wheat with goat's milk and cardamom
raga bhairavi, shimmering jazz
renata tebaldi's legs wrapped around
verdi. poems that bloom like roadside daisies:

jane hirshfield, kabir, mirabai
                    basho. rumi

white lilies in a blue vase
my fingers like warm wax around the barrel
of this pen; lined paper beaded with the
mercury of my heart. the peace of things—
their comfort, silently offered, their patient
giving. round plates with red and yellow rims
cobalt cups, hot as the kiln which fired them
the perfect heft of stainless steel forks
shallow ponds of spoons. the beauty—the
sturdy, honest beauty of things, ungelded
by tricks of light on water, innocent
of tidal undertow

i say no to plunder and papayas
ripped from their beds at midnight, the black pearls
of their seeds crushed under careless feet. no
to raids on houses of the poor who must
lick their honey off the edge of a razor
blade. no to revenge; no to seductions
that ring like crystal goblets stained ruby-red
with the wine of entitlement. i bite
the hand that reaches for cream without passing
the coffee. i say no
to arguments about angels dancing
on the heads of pins. angels have better
things to do—tend to plants and babies
mothers and turtles, those who stay home
move slowly, live close to the ground. who do
not expect the universe to throw them
a meteor shower to celebrate every
changed diaper or the patient laying
and hatching of eggs. I say no to clutched
fists and fires that feed on stolen fuel. no
to being buried in the Department
of Home Furnishings at Sears. no.

Every no bears in its belly the sibilant
yes: a pomegranate seed white in its
sheath of translucent red

On the balcony of our house in Bombay,
my mother grew dragons in pots. Their
shimmering heads emerged from dark soil,
wobbled on delicate necks, grew muscular,
breathed gusts of fire. Their scales were iridescent,
light shimmered in peacock folds on their backs.

Eventually, they smashed the pots with their tails,
their leathery wings opcned and they flew
around the house, hovered above the balcony,
settled on the terrace. At night they slept
under my bed. One dragon had a tongue
of silver. One breathed gold. One scorched my
eyebrows when he laughed. One bit a hole

in my heart, planted a dragon seed, which
grew and grew. Now a baby dragon flicks
its tail between my shoulder-blades, between
the shadow and its whisper:

wings, wings

Ashem vohu, vahishtem asti
Ushta asti, ushta ahmai

Standing beside Zarthustra's
portrait, facing the rising sun, my father
chants prayers. Zarthustra's eyes look up to
heaven. My father's eyes are closed. Sunlight
burnishes his face. I think my father
is more handsome than Zarthustra. I think
my father is god. This love that blooms in my chest
is god.

Shekaste, shekaste shaitan. My father
flicks the whip of his *kustee* behind him,
drives the Evil One back. With his words,
he banishes the dark. I believe in
the power of his words. I believe

Lying on my back on the verandah
of our summer home in Khandala.
Overhead, the sky is warm, purple-black
and plump, like *jamun* berries, swimming with stars.

I'm in love with night. Floating up into
the circle of the Seven Sisters, my
cheek scrapes against Orion's belt. Dragon
wings spread. The right wing casts its shadow
over Asia; the left, just beginning
to grow, is a painful nub of tender
light. The night sky is God. This
wordless love
is God.

You gods and bearded prophets, go squabble
in the pub for a while. I've heard enough
of heroes and lightning chariots streaking
across the sky. My companions are Tara
and Devi. They cook with me and wash
dishes afterwards. This chipped blue bowl
into which I dip my spoon is the
goddess's face. The hand, which caresses—
its tendons and veins and miraculous
fingers—works her threads of light into
muscular days. I kneel to scrub the floor.

Night stretches around me like a giant
balloon. Thirty-four, and my nightgown
smells of sour milk. My first-born cries and will
not sleep. My mouth tastes of dead fish. Dark as
jamun berries are my son's eyes, wide open

as night sky. *Ashem vahu*, I chant into
his perfect ear, *vahishtem asti*. This
exhausted love, is it god? My son, my
perfect wailing son

Fifty-two. Body aches—burning back,
grinding hip, throbbing ankle—speak to me.
I reply: *yes, tell me;* or love ...
I say, *how about a hot bath?*

No longer lie on my back on the
balcony. No longer swim in the night
sky.

Om tara tuttare
        the goddess rises.

Star, evening star

Heart's small voice sings
we

    us

        this

            yes!

Heart wears itself on its own sleeve; it
delights in slippery mud and fallen petals.
It kisses Head's myriad grey pleats and
great, furrowed brow. Head mutters: *you*

time-waster, mooner, you singer who can't
reach high c; mistake-maker, incontinent
bleeder; giver of gifts you cannot
afford; blissed-out, undiscriminating,
lacerated fool

Yes! sings heart

    bird

       flower

          rock

            fish

               star

   starfishrockbirdflower!

Show me in your emerald heart, in the
current of your river. Show me how
to open my hands, your laughing light
trembling between my palms.

     Tara, show me

I have left the house with no roof. Hands ache
from clutching water, gripping air. No
ground, no walls, no rooms. I have left them all
behind. See my boat leak. See the boatman
return to our ruined village. My clothes

left on the river bank. I don't know how
to swim, how

     I have forgotten my name

RISHMA DUNLOP

Photo by Joseph Paczuski

The poetic impulse is a seeking of dialogue with otherness, with language, form, emotion and ideas all commensurate. For me, poetry is the desire to touch something undeniable, an attempt to express what is withheld from knowing. The poem is a gesture toward the deep image, what we know as primordial, a locus for rhythm, music, cadence. The poem is a form of prayer, an act of faith, attuned to grace and sacred conversation with another. Writing poetry is a redemptive movement toward the culturally incorrect, the strange, the ineffable. The poet, in order to read and write mindfully, must become a cultural outsider. Writing poetry requires a stubborn practice for which there is no definitive guidebook, no map.

The Poet Contemplates Her Art

But where my moment of Brocade—
My—drop—of—India?
—Emily Dickinson

What have I expected poetry to do for me? At midlife, poetry has not yielded a God. Poetry is that unfinished thing, some intangible hope. Persistent practice of courage. It is the waiting for a loved one to return home. It is the young woman I was. It is the hue of my wedding sari, shot silk the color of dawn, brocade border of gold. Not the usual red silk of the Indian bride, some whisper of hope contained there in my rebellion. As the light fades, the mind wanders over books, pen and paper, even as the hour pulls you into exhaustion. What a scrap of paper gives . . . a grocery list, letters, the 2 AM fevered composition, Cicero's memory palaces, Book of the Dead. Raw faith in the light of another day, in public records, private histories, the poet unfurling poems like Tibetan prayer flags or the prayers the Japanese tie to trees. The air above the city is saturated with poets' prayers, like the air of industrial towns and dreams, so thick with longing it is hard to breathe. And what resides in the ink but a glimpse of the possible past in memory as you turn off the light, the possible years left to you written, recorded, your hands a reliquary.

Ancestors

I hear them behind me in another continent
                              across the Indian Ocean
crossing the floors, soft sweep of sandals
in my mother's country. I was born there four
decades ago at 2 AM. My birth certificate reads
One Living Female Child.

Today my passport reads Nationality: Canadian.

My mother's land is still there
scooters and rickshaws navigating through crowded streets
full of billboards for Bollywood films,
dreamscapes of floating lotus ponds
lush public gardens, the smells of decay and sweet jasmine,
still the bustling bazaars and stinking alleyways,
cities like Victorian London among palm trees and banyans,
the rivers marking the routes of cranes and egrets.

The ancestors are still there, with the last remnants of the
                                         British Raj
drinking chai scented with cardamom
old women in desert white saris,
turbanned sirdars,

the young women with amber skin, hair and brows as black
as crows wings, eyes of lionesses in heat,
dressed in silks of delirious hues, violent pinks,
                    bangles and anklets clinking

they wander through foreign rooms
        in the last daylight of the century
painting their eyes
brush of sandalwood across the collarbone.

Somewhere out of them, alive or dead I have sprung
yet no one seems to recognize me.

No one.

First Lessons: Postcolonial

At Briarwood Elementary,
we stood at attention in our Oxford shoes,
navy tunics, white blouses with novitiate collars,
spines stiffened to the strains of singing
God Save the Queen to the Union Jack
recited The Lord's Prayer
hallowed be thy name, learned lessons
from a Gideon's bible.

In geography and history lessons
the teacher would unroll the giant map
of the world from the ceiling, use her
wooden pointer to show the countries
of the Empire, the slow spread of a faded
red stain that marked them, soft burgundy
like the colour of my father's turbans.
Ancient history. Crisp whites of cricket
matches at officers' clubs. Afternoon tea
in the pavilion.

Decades later I can reconstruct
the story, move past the pink glow,
excavate the hollows of history.

If that surface was scratched
the pointer would fly along the contours of
the parchment world, across the Himalayas,
through emerald coils of steaming rivers.
Under my fingernails, the scents of spices
and teas, the silk phrasings of my mother's
saris, the stench of imperial legacy, blood
spilled from swords on proper khaki uniforms
lanced through the bodies of Sikh soldiers at
the frontlines of her Majesty's British Army.

But our teacher never said: *Remember this.*

Anthem

1

Place your hands that I love upon me.
Say my name as prayer. Taste each
brine sweet syllable. This is what will
haunt us. Stone hearts in our mouths.
Your love will not be salvation.
This I know.

2

Watch me burn. The cells of my old body
melt away. Bracelet my wrists with your grip.
Drink the blue that rivers my hands. Make my bones
lovely.

3

Meet the rush of my wants, meet the
light of outrage, the after-burn. Edgelit.

4

Language is always culpable. Grammar
a climate of love. Write in the colors of a
Tintoretto dusk. Slice of moon, scrape of sky,
armfuls of rain. Read me with conviction, absolute.
Fit your words to me like the precise cut
of tuxedo, riding jacket, Dior gown.

5

Take every journey into the past,
delusions, false namings of events.
Take memory that gnaws on the ribs and
turn it into prophecy. Revise me until brave
new days bloom in my throat.

6

Love me. Cradle me in gentleness.
Release the heart's shroud. Make me the
last poem in your book. Let me hear you say
I want this more than anything. This love will
not save us. I would run from it but it is the
only grace. *Love. Lean into its slant.* Postscript
of light in every century.

Naramata Road

You know this is a landscape that tends to unfasten
you, brings you again and again to the brink of weeping.

No matter how many departures and disappearances,
you are marked by this beauty, astonishment that depends on loss.

As the bitter edges of things slide into memory and flesh, you
claim the meaning of your days on this frayed loveliness.

You sign your name to it.

At these moments something is given back to you, panic
dusted off, calmed by desert heat in the summer, vineyards

heavy with grapes. The body is set to music, carried by rain in
the spring resurrection of orchards. In the fall, the road swells with

harvest, the ripe comfort of apples. Even in winter, the skeletons of
trees dangle gifts, Golden Delicious earrings abandoned to the wind.

The ghosts of dead teenagers and drunks live here, their
voices echo along the curves and bends, in the rocky incisions of

graves, haunted by memories of prom dresses, cigarettes smoked in
the Seven Eleven parking lot and behind the high school.

There is a soft spot in everything.

You drive that road, move into a sky like a late Turner painting, gold
and amber, white canvas dreaming colors of Venice. It makes you believe

there is tenderness in every geography. And this has the power to change you,
unweight your eyelids every morning, as the sky leans towards the absolute.

Augustinian Heart

We talk about art and its source
of greatness.
How a painting or poem could move you like
a religious impulse, spirit and matter infused,
true and beautiful.
Year after year each time you read that poem, or
see that painting, a still-life, a self-portrait,
an abstract landscape so loved by the artist
you ache to touch it, to hold it.

————

We talk into the night.
Behind the house, the crescent moon silvers
the wilderness dark.
In the flesh of my hand—the knowledge of your flesh:
all I need; all I know.

If art is a private religion, so is love. We take it all to heart,
as if, Augustine said, our existence depends upon our having loved.
Beauty so ancient and so new.

We try to tell each other about the sacred
what needs to be visible to the jaded eye.

————

The long slow walk leads us back to each other.
Winter air frosts our bones and our cold arms are full
of each other and the everyday immortal ache of spirit for matter,
of matter for spirit.
I have come to understand this is the same need
grasped through the lips   hands   body and in the
vision that if we touch what we love, if we hold it,
behold it, then it will last.

Reading Anna Karenina

The volume of Tolstoy thumbs her open.
She tries to keep the heroine alive.

Outside the library windows
ragged moths beat against the streetlamps.
She feels the heat of locomotive steam
rising from the stacks, weeps when she
sees Anna's red purse on the tracks.

She closes the book with stunned hands
as if she had touched the hem of a final
morning, a sense of that going into it alone.
She begins to think she will not be carried
unscarred, untorn into any heaven. Wants
someone to hold her while she burns.

Saccade

The chronicle of the city unravels
                              like a prayer cloth
calm of storybook nurseries, book codes,
swift calligraphy of desire.

The city dreams us
                gives us exigencies in eavesdropped
                stories, undistinguished pleadings
                requiems for forgetting.

There is a small star pinned where Hiroshima used to be.

It's late and someone's almost forgotten how to convince you
                                        he's telling the truth.
Even in sleep he cries out for help
                and you minister to him
                a woman like history returning for its wounded.

Blackbirds drop from telephone wires
                        rose petals collect in birdbaths.

————

Everything stories you. You take Rilke at his word.
Taste it everywhere. Wonderland signs
                        Eat me. Drink me.

Your hands like hobbled birds
read the classics. The hero enters the arched gate of the city.
In these books it is clear where the story of the city begins.

In the book of lost entries
                nothing is pure but the forgotten things
crossed out words on a haunted page
                        useless dark of ink.

————

Today the city is unwriting itself
                        in a coffin of glass.

In the blurred doorways,
                     in skyscrapers that rise silver and blue
cool as if nothing could ever make them burn.

Sprayed on concrete walls
Where is my beautiful daughter
Emma was here
Escúchame
I'll pray for you Lucas
Fuck the politicians
Recuérdame
Inamorata

         the billboard with the women tall
         with long legs against white sand and blue ocean
         red mouths puckered high above the crowds
smooth lipsticked smiles longing for cigarettes and sex.

         ———

Across the city, lights are shutting off
Good night, good night.

On the radio, the sirens are singing
Emily Lou Harris, Alison Kraus, Gillian Welch
ethereal lullaby *Didn't Leave Nobody But the Baby*

Come lay your bones
on the alabaster stones
and be my ever-lovin'baby.

Reading Emily Dickinson
                   Beauty crowds me til I die
You feel the loneliness.
That's what is left of the dream of beauty.

Beauty
         So many kinds to name.

You hope for a day soft at the edges
                for something, someone to
                know the small hands of rain
to be like rain
wet with a decent happiness.

———

Kiss the gleaming armor of the world.
Feel its electric purr.
Close your hands on wind-stunned leaves.
Buff the scars of history with your mouth.

KULDIP GILL

It is unusual for me to think of the theory, art or science of my poetry or the nature and function of that poetry. I've rarely been asked to note or explain the types, forms and techniques that appear in my "corpus of poetry" to date. A cursory glance shows a poet who is in a liminal place between the two tendencies of romanticism and classicism. The first shows in my poems that are emotional, inspirational and personal (see the use of "I" and "me") in which an organic structure or form is apparent. The latter is apparent in more structured and carefully crafted verses (ghazals, sonnets, glosas) that depend more on an image or images and perhaps less tendency to use the "I" and "me" forms to communicate insights. Throughout, I try to understand our world as I write about the various types of diaspora (traditionalists, assimilationists and integrationists), exiles and expatriates, the dominant society and its economic, political and social attributes. Issues of "home" and environment (India, where I was born, the Fraser Valley where I was raised, Vancouver where I live, and the places where I've traveled), immigration, and hybridity, all have a fundamental and intended impact on what I write. Overall, these complex issues: including gender, ethnicity, personal experiences, didactic interests, my instructors and colleagues, and all the poets I read, on whose shoulders I stand, influence my poetry.

Everywoman's life. Shall I call her,
that is each woman, by name or
shall I call them all, She?
—Mina Loy

Ghazal I

You smell impure, she says of women. She eats its ashes—
the fire flies in all directions. Her lips burn. There are no children.

Not yet fifteen. Lured to cross the kala pani. The penalty
ten linked chains and a cacophony of imbeciles: indenture.

Into whose paradises, whose hells? The white seers, blue sugar canes.
Fijians in the kava ritual drunk beyond apparent logic, mockery's fair game.

The evil 'lines' and the rarity of women.
Caan and Abel without rival. Fiji jungles of Methodists.

The farm life, a meld of caste, fish in boxes, those 'tins'. Nadala leaves.
Large bunches of dried grasses, to keep head lice from the bed.

A toddler tied to her mother's cot, kept from the well
by the reach of her invalid's switch. A father lives a spell, tourist hells.

Bhachma's Musings

Ghazal II

She swings to and fro: identity to icon, and back. Her lies.
She pumps her feet caste to caste blue skying with friends.

Girmitya, a noble mask of oneself, the collective memory.
The other portrait a tracery, the overseer's whips' lines: doubts, fears.

I was eleven when I got married and came here. In Nasavu, I stayed
for three or four years. Sometimes I liked it. Sometimes I did not.

I have to stay with my husband even if I have difficulties,
I rati, rati. I had a baby girl, a child—I had them every three years.

Language? the teacher says, "The lingua franca here is Fiji-Hindi.
We try for a coherent discourse." She says that. We call it Fiji-bat.

Ghazal III

An improvised hammock: a mosquito net swings a small infant in it.
Hurricane came, everything flew—inside one room, eight of us were living.

Nigel and Eric. There was nothing like Oscar. Three hurricanes—
see my water tank. Eight of us inside it when the house roof blew away.

My husband died. I had a man BP as my Dharam ke Bhai. Fijians came.
I wasn't afraid. Cannibals? No three-pronged forks for brains.

Yes they could have kahlata us. I don't like fighting.
Ki mafit rahta ra: I lived freely among them. I was a widow then.

I faced a lot of difficulties, and still face a lot.
I don't know when I will have some ease: Kub sook mili.

On the boat I paid 10 cents for parathas. Insects were in the food.
He made the four of us sit together. We took tea, drank and ate paratha as ek sath.

Go to India? I write letters. There is no one there to answer. My message to my
mother: she should not take comfort from waiting for me: humari assara ne karo.

Four O'clock Tea at Harrison Hot Springs Hotel:

The chairs leaned up against the glass table
covered by an opaque white umbrella
the patio empty except at our window
where we sit over cups of tea and a square
of chocolate cake clinging on the saucer's edge.
A glass globe hangs outside and is
suddenly assailed by a hummingbird—
No! There are at least three, and one
hovers, waits its turn at the sweet red
water blossoms. I am reminded of Delhi,
the Uberoi hotel, tea on the grounds, the white
and red turbaned waiters bringing trays of
tea and thin cucumber sandwiches as we sat
in the shade along the edges of the lawn.
When I was four, and seven twittering
birds landed nearby, my mother
explained they are called satht-bai—
the seven brothers, since they travel as
a small flock. Travelers, like us.

Mrs. Spilsbury at the Plough—Whonnock, 1911

Cedar trees, two rows
of twenty-three upright four-by-sixes frame
the Spilsbury house in black outline against the sky.
Four props assist the house until the house is built.
Uncut logs lay strewn across the yard and down the hill.
Mrs. Spilsbury holds a set of reins and he, the handles
of the plough. The two horses pull, their feet planted,
necks arched, as they roll over another furrow of rocks,
earth and mangled root bundles. Sikh men watch, stopped
in their tracks by Mrs. Spilsbury in white blouse, straw hat
and long skirt, as she stalks along the furrow shouting
Gee Hah! as she slaps the reins on the horses' flanks.

The four turbaned men stand relaxed,
their arms hang loose from their shoulders, perhaps
astounded by her resolve. They have propped up *Spilsbury
House.* The studs stand straight up on either side of the floor,
leveled with one side flush on the ground, the other raised
and supported by a foundation of upright logs. It is nineteen
hundred and eleven. Four Sikhs in coveralls stand watch
at Mrs. Spilsbury and her team at the plough.

Another Sunday in August

Just as we round the corner, the field's
    mown grass is visible as green-brown
        stubble. The burnt house has weathered

another winter, its sun-browned stomach shines
    in the sun as if still tanning and the swallows dipped
        in the pond-side mud, swerve to miss the electric lines,

unafraid of the men still mowing this end of the farm
    while the old farmer, nicknamed *Cadthu,* or pumpkin
        when young, scratches his head, cap in hand, talking

to the yawning tenant, about the thefts from his trailers,
    that are unending, linked stories by an unseasoned novelist,
        and he muses that they never catch 'em at it, still everyone

except him has seen 'em. While at the cottage his teenage daughters
    and a friend stand at the tap, washing their legs and arms of wet clay
        caking their skin and Nikes, as she tells them of what it was

like during that fieldwork year in Fiji. The muddy fields,
    her thongs caked, and sari raised around her knobby knees
        going to a village wedding all wet earth, field dirtied.

Homage to a Frieze

Wound around, stone.
No, it wraps and winds its way around the temple.
These women with their mango breasts and ample hips,
still and looking boldly at you and me, voyeurs
for centuries. Khujaraho.

French Lace

She was just home from the hospital,

as I went in she looked up at me

pulled back the sheet that covered

her chest, the scar where one breast

used to be. She smiled, shy, sleepily

told me that her surgeon is a woman

who loves needle work; who makes

fine laces, and embroideries. "And this is mine,

the surgeon made it for me," she said proudly.

She can see the gash with its redness

and brittle threads as the finest French Val lace

with baby beading, or French Maline, single loop

tatting, or other open-work and tracery. Perhaps

it is. Fearlessly, I looked

at its exquisiteness.

And already in its dark grove
the train is waiting with its breath of ashes
—Louise Glück

Sonnets for My Father—(three from a 'crown' of seven sonnets)

I

I remember that day, it was six. I lived in town.
I'd come home from the office tired and drained.
Suddenly: A *panic*. I was beside my bed, sunk down
on my knees. Me, who never thought of it, prayed.

Oh! God what is this feeling? What is this *knowing*?
I thought of the plane—they were flying to Germany.
Something's wrong. What is it? An angel warning.
The phone rang. Even in its cradle—it tolled gethsemane.

The kind of calls we fear most. Was it them?
My youngest brother said, come home right away.
What's wrong? Kuldip, it's Daddy. The doctor, then
on the line, said, Kuldip, your father's sick, today . . .

Replied, yes, when I asked, *is he in the hospital?*
Said, *come home right away—do you drive at all?*

II

He said, *come home right away—do you drive at all?*
What has happened. What has happened? I was afraid
it would be about a plane gone down. But that call
was about my Dad. My Dad? That moment I stayed

frozen on the edge of the bed then as a whirlwind
I flew around, readied myself, to go home. To my dad.
I was always needed in times like these. We send
for the eldest. I had to see for myself how sick he was, how bad.

It seemed to take hours to drive home to Mission.
Excruciatingly slowly the valley passed by my window.
At times someone at the side of the road, an illusion,
I thought could be my brother Stanley (or some foe?)

standing car-less, unable to go home to what waited
keep going. These *things* tried to tell me something, conveyed

III

keep going. These *things* tried to tell me something, conveyed
to us. It took nerve to drive by, to tell myself, *no it's not*
my younger brothers. I knew they too had the message relayed.
Some message. I read it—but wrong. *My heart on a blue stalk.*

Home. The men stood: crossed arms, in front of the house.
Uncles, neighbours, other men who came to us, grieving
too, in our grieving. My brave middle brother, his spouse
carrying his first child. My father only saw the conceiving

mother-to-be, not his grandchild, their first baby. He was gone
too soon. Now Kal, the eldest boy got the turban of succession
the men came to put it on his head as the firstborn son.
As an adult he'd never worn one. His hair shorn when he was seven.
He was brave. He saw that I couldn't bear to see my father dead.
Tenderly: *It's ok, you can go and see Daddy,* my brother said,

Almost a Glosa—for Jim

The darkness lifts, imagine, in your lifetime.
There you are—cased in clear bark you drift
Through weaving rushes, fields flooded with cotton.
You are free. The river films with lilies,
—Louise Glück, "The Undertaking"

Did you imagine how far we'd travel? Us.
The day we met, sitting across the table
from each other at Moishe's? You across
from her, and me from him. They talked.
We smiled, then you called. At that time
I doubted anyone could be so kind. Imagine.
We are wont to pull in against the tides.
But, above that we've managed to
undertake us. Our lives. See—shapes shift.
There you are—cased in clear bark you drift

along. A hot sun blazed through windows of a blue buick.
Miles of green scent rising from lines of rutted furrows
seeped up from the ground into the car.
From somewhere—the synapses or amygdala,
came the call of memory. I knew it—the smell acrid,
nostalgic. My mother's hands full of white cotton.
She walked in, vanished, reappeared, through unripe
recall. Plato's tabula abrasa. Now in the valley
near San Jose, or was it Fresno? Back in Faridkot?
Through weaving rushes, fields flooded with cotton.

You are free. The river films with lilies, the far bank
shallow. The chortling stream flows over white
rocks, grey flecked granite. Hard and unforgiving
though they seem. A place to dangle our feet and sit
in wonder. It seems that we have come far, near
to be in this place. The peace. *I have survived my life.*
Drive on, it will be hours yet before we stop to rest.
The road winds down river banks, edges of arroyos.
There, see? The moon's long rays on water frills.
You are free. The river films with lilies.

SONNET L'ABBÉ

Why do I write poetry? Fear—warded off by leaving marks in the physical world. *Rage*—to decry witnessed and lived injustice. *Awe*—a word is only a sound, attached to the real by threads of mutual agreement. *Rebellion*—we to the laws of syntax are subject(s). *Vanity*—to give this given name my own meaning. *Communion*—why is red passion, white purity, black death? *Loneliness*—from the depth of the body's solitude, light just wants to radiate and be seen. *Question/Answer*—is a beautiful equilibrium of breath. *Moment*—but O! language takes place in time. *Celebration*—the Cosmos doesn't bloom to get paid.

Killarnoe

Killarnoe is a place I just invented right
now. I just built it from my head. I started
with a letter k and set down the letters
that spilled out. What does that say when k-i-l-l

first sprouts? Something repressed, or
an instinct, that when allowed a moment's
free reign, it opens to its own mind
and speaks bluntly? But see how I persisted

past the first impulse to slash at the page's
clean white throat, and instead adorned it
with a pretty vowel, gently drawing out the ells
to sulk the k down into a rumbled,

grudging argument against the mind's knee-
jerk proposal, the oh opening to compromise,
and a silent e watching without judgment.
Killarnoe, I decide, is the land

of our ancient people.

Bi-Polarity

The long tertiary function
of my mood. Three axes:
space, moment, matter.

One arm reaches
along a gaseous blissness
the other approaches
the hardest nothingful hole.

The stupid numeracy
of the heartbeat's series,
the arbitrary meaning
of xx, xy.

Sleeping bodies
hard driven
by the boolean beat
of ones and ohs, in me

the Fibonacci conscience
wakes weeping, shakes
the fractal, nervous
core geometry.

Water rises to the surface,
I apply the cold poultice
of rational logic, try to
freeze the ebb and flow,

but now yes, now no:
I think, therefore I think I know,
but am probably
just a Libran aggregate

dwelling on
the dangerous pore
of the origin.

Tone

is an important aspect
of any class text. Ask
your professor if you may
say *no way!* to object, or
hey! to interject, in any essay
meant to earn respect.

You can't say: *this dude*
knows his shit. Nor can you
say: *he's full of it*. To argue
your point, your joint
gotta have vocab game.

However and *nonetheless*
kick *but*'s ass. They got
up-in-front-of-the class.
Address to impress.
Your convention hall pass.

The rules of tone are all
unspoken. One learns
the hard way
that they can be broken.

My Osama Bin Laden T-Shirt

It sits in the drawer.
What is it for?
What is it for?

See how blue his eyes are?
The benevolent, Christ-like smile?
Above his head, his turban
curves a clean white halo glow.

On the back, a night-vision
through rifle's sights:
the pair of towers caught within
a pale green circle on black—
America Under Attack!

I bought it in Korea.
A man under an overpass
was selling US army surplus
out of the back of a truck.

It came home at the bottom
of my suitcase. No wands
nor x-rays picked it up.

One Halloween,
Jerry wore it under a green flak jacket
and an embroidered Uzbek cap.
I dressed in my own brown skin, in silk hijab
and a kaftan I got at Goodwill.

Young men eyed us on the streetcar.
I had Jerry button his coat.
Suddenly naked in public
with that scarf around my head.

At the party, people I'd never met
didn't know I was dressed up.
Are you John Walker Lindh?
they asked Jerry.

We stood together and waved
the little American flags
we bought in Chinatown.

We're Americans, we said.

It's the same old joke.
No costume equals serial killer.
Get it? We look just like everyone else?

—

The tag says:
Care on Reverse.

The universal symbols:
X over the iron,
X over the bleach.

Despite the warnings
I machine washed it.
Tumbled it dry.

It survived.

—

My Osama Bin Laden
T-shirt
sits in the drawer.
What is it for?
Will it ever get worn out?

I don't think that kind
brown face can see
the light of day.

So sometimes I sleep in it.
Sometimes I pray.

Waves

we are waves the mass radiation
we are waves the masculinear desire
we are waves in space an atom/ically
we are waves the plasmability of fire

we are waves amid the spill of liquid
we are waves through the chill crystal trees
we are waves on an ebonymy of absence
we are waves above the lightened normalties

we are waves the spring of the coil sprung
we are waves the wire's stubborn heart
we are waves the emblematic war's begun
we are waves the circularity of art

Theory, My Natural Brown Ass

I've paid for too many degrees,
posited too many historical positions,
made too many semiotic apologetics,
forwarded far too many feminist responses
to too many textual materialities

to have an ass this big.

In theory, my ass
does not signify.

But this insistence of the body,
this non-linguistic expression
of inertia and caloric lust,
is a corporeal truth that mental exercise
can't deconstruct.

Or is it just an inverted absence?
The presence of the lack
of any Aryan heritage?

I'm the post-colonial girl
who went abroad and squatted and lunged
while the maid, snapping out
wet laundry, watched.
Skinny brown bitch, was what I thought!
The poor men looked at my ass
like it was a pair of Boston Cremes.

But I was raised
on white girls' dreams.
This juicy back might fly in hip hop,
but I meant to fit
into tinier social circles,
and JLo's butt's already taking up
two stools at the representation bar.
Missy E's already gone
bonh bo bonh bonh
all the way to the bank.

My ass doesn't give a shit
that my mind is post third wave.
It is imperialist, a booty-Gap,
expanding into a third space: the place

beyond my seams. Who cares
that sizes are all 'seems' anyway:
you shop, you walk
the slippery significatory slope
on which an 'S', 'M' or 'L' might fall.
The mall

is the spatial organization
of desire, I know, but
does that make my ass look small?

Open Letter

I want to offer my apologies
to you, whoever you are.

You don't know me.
Right now you're trying to get free
of a cage whose bars
are belief or pain or immediate need,
probably aiming your justified rage
at someone closer,
someone visible, or if there are
no moving targets within your range
then inward, where your anger
will fling its tiny arrows
all along the bloody corridors
of intestines, nerves and veins.

I want to say I'm sorry
for all the ways I keep you there.
For all the days I reach
for more than my share.
Everyone here has more than theirs,
so that a smaller more seems poor.
We don't compare our shares
to yours.

I can't undo what's been done
by those who came before.
Please know I stone myself
with hard words
like 'cog' or 'whore.'

If I had the key, I'd send it.
"Make copies for your friends!"

Instead I hope it helps to say:
equilibrium does keep score.
Have mercy, I know
your cage isn't imagined.

Imagination is its door.

From "Dumb Animal"

Uh

The shyness, the delay to say
I'm thinking, I'm processing,
the silence before the words
string into coherence I can't leave
unfilled, all my ignorance,
the mice scurrying in the maze,
please wait while the images
load, sound saying I'm not dumb

or the coyness, the delay to say
I'm answering, when I'm processing
the first thought into a string of words
less hurtful, less assessing,
less revealing of the blunt fact
of my unkindness, all my interiority,
the scurry to hide it behind my back
please wait while I remember
your heart, sound the safety on a sharp
tongue

Oh

(((((O)))))

this o is my throat
this o is my oh yeah
this o is my really
this o is my credulousness

((((O))))

this o is my soundful closed
this o is my politeness
this o is my mask
this o is my feigned interest

(((O)))

this o is my I see
this o is the shared place
this o is my sympathy
this o is my mistake

((o))

this o is my aha
this o is my incredulousness
this o is my startling backward
this o is our otherness

(o)

this o is just o
this o is symbolic sound
this o is the presence of nothing
this o is common ground

o

this o is my lips
this o is my gentle kiss
this o is my suckling
o my greedy tenderness

oh
uh-oh
oh

Danielle Lagah

I do not speak my father's native language: instead, I write poems. Like any child of an immigrant parent I have struggled to belong to two worlds and have often failed; it has been through writing that I have at length found an authentic method of connection with my heritage. The work included in this anthology represents a small portion of my pursuit to unearth and preserve the stories of one immigrant family; it is my desire that through this pursuit I will also come to reach some understanding of my own cultural identity. I've been asked many times to explain why poetry is the most appropriate genre through which to tell these stories, and the answer is not without complexity. The stories themselves are fragmented—pieces of information and details gathered from many places and people. There are mislaid events and gaps of missing time that pure prose could never hope to bridge—fiction seems too concrete, too linear, somehow too much of an invention. John Hollander once said that "we can reclaim truth from the lies of poetry," and in this I believe he is correct. My poems are crafted from thick layers of perception and fabrication, but it is my hope that these layers serve to illuminate and protect the truths at their core. These are my truths, and my father's truths, and on the page they at last share a common tongue.

Glossary of Terms

chuni—long scarf traditional in Indian dress
jalahbia—bright orange sweet in concentrated sugar syrup
lardu—large, round flour sweet
packora—battered and deep-fried vegetable and/or meat
roti—flatbread
saag—curry dish made with spinach and paneer
surma—eye kohl
tandoor—brick/clay oven

Glossary of Characters (in relation to the narrator)

Aaj—uncle
Piara—father
Piari*—aunt
Shivani—grandmother
Tage—aunt

* These poems are part of a book-length series recounting the history of an immigrant family. Earlier poems in the series describe how, at the age of seven, Piari was mysteriously poisoned in the family's village of Pubwan.

Dolls

Shivani (Mother):

When I was a girl
I made dolls. Collected
fabric scraps from under my mother's
bench, snagged the bright bits
from her old saris before
she used them as rags. Once
I found a piece of machete blade in the wheat field
and tried to cut up my auntie's best red *chuni*
the one that was the color of Bombay lips. My hands
were too small to use a dull blade on silk
I dropped the tatters into the well so she
would never know, watched them fall into the darkness
like red kisses

In the shade of houses the village girls sat
in half-circles, away from the boys. Working our bent needles
our coarse black thread. We stitched doll faces, mouths
upturned lines of closed smiles. Wove yarn
into *surma* around the eyes. Dancing dresses
in purples and golds, skirts
that twirled up around cotton legs. Once
a boy came running into us, chasing
a wheel rim, his bare chest
heaving. He stumbled and
grasped my shoulder, laughing. Broke
our circle

That was the year that my grandmother
kept me from school, her eyes on me
in the kitchen while I pounded dough. *Not
enough hard,* she told me, *your fingers
too weak.* She whispered about men, her voice
like a dull blade through silk. Gave me
a pot of *surma,* black as thread. I watched
friends pass my window on their way to school
new dolls in their hands
I pulled up water from the well for tea, waited
to pull up kisses

Untitled

A farmer saw Piari often on the outskirts of the mango grove weeks after she had died. The first time he glimpsed her it was still monsoon, the rain too heavy for his eyes to navigate the drops; he half thought she was a lost bull calf. He swung his head back and forth like a peacock in heat, held his hands in front of him as though he could part the storm. He rode his buffalo toward her blurred image and it was afraid to go.

It was months later that he bolted into the village, eyes so strange it was like they had melted from staring at intense heat, so that the colors began to run, brown into white. He'd been gone for three nights, telling his wife he would sleep under the sky now that the rains had passed. When he came running Piara and Aaj were walking the wall by the pond. They watched him get closer, his legs kicking up in the tall grass, red tunic sliding off of his shoulders. A piece of iron chain in his hand, swinging. They watched for the thing that must be chasing him to appear—the flash of a long tooth, the wink of a stripe. A forked tongue.

He came to them screaming, rousing sleeping cows. He described her face, her throat swollen with poison, peaking out from around a mango tree. Her eyes beckoning. *She curls on my chest in the night,* he howled, *I wake up and cannot get a breath. It is like so many stones.*

The village seers grasped him by the arms, dragged him to Piari's grave. They meant to beat him with the iron chain to loose her spirit. *It is no good,* he said. *I have already beaten myself.* They lifted off his shirt to see the blood, pooling in the link marks on his back. He stayed there, writhing on her grave through the night. Sometimes he called her name, like a lover's.

Piari's Cremation

Aaj (Brother):

    I was too young when she died
    but I remember they always
    told you not to look
    too hard at the fire, or
    the souls of the burning dead would enter
    through your eyes

Piara:

    I must've seen her
    burning at the cremation site
    I can't remember but I must've
    they always made you watch
    that kind of thing

Her Cremation Did Not Face the Rising Sun

One year after
Piari was burned
my father
lay shaking with fever in his straw bed, the heat
rubbing against his skin
like bristling tiger hair. He
spoke strange
vowels. Bugs crawled
over his chest, black and green.

Holy men came to the house,
laid their hands on him. Their eyes
rolled back. My grandmother dropped
coins into their white beards, dirty
tunic bibs
Piari's spirit is fevered, they told her
Her cremation did not face the rising sun, the ashes
backward in the earth, so now
she cannot rest

    In my dreams I have seen her
    beyond the wall
    where they burned her
    pulling at singed hair, wiping
    the green stains from her mouth, so scared
    She slips in
    to my father's chest and hides there
    cleans the poison still on her tongue
    with his blood

Men from the village exhumed the entire
patch of ground that had mixed
with her remains. Turned it
like a straw mattress and set it down again
seamless in the earth. My grandmother
sat cross-legged in her veils, my father
laid out across her lap
and watched the sun rise

Two Stories of Mudfish

Aaj (Brother):

In the pond by the mango grove were mudfish, slick and dark, long as my arm. We spent the afternoons down there trying to catch one, brown clouds of silt under our kicking legs. That was before I could touch the bottom, when Piara would dive down and come back clutching handfuls of pond weed, swearing he had touched a fin, held a tail. I wouldn't put my face in then, not even when Piari threw a thin glass bangle into the water and told me to get it back; I watched dumbly while it slipped below the surface, shining and green

After, when she died, I went back. Dove in again and again, my fingers searching through the thick muck, fish touching me from all around. I found marbles, orange peels, the bones of a dog. Her bracelet was gone, stuck in the belly of a fish or buried too deep

Piara:

Once when I was sick Aaj brought a fish in the house, one of the ones from the pond with the back fins and long whiskers. I remember him standing in the doorway of the bedroom, brown water dripping from his hair, his shorts. Making a big puddle on the floor. He had it tight in both hands, holding it up like a sword for me to see, his eyes bright and serious. *Ec tdar orna, Piara, I got one*

My mother turned to look and dropped her bowl full of yogurt, screamed so loud that Auntie came running down from the tandoor on the roof. I remember the two of them squealing, feet stamping around like in a dance, jewelry flashing, their hands wild. And Aaj's laugh, the sound of it rushing through the house like cool water
soothing my fever

Her Place

Shivani (Mother):

> *The Taj Mahal has rooms below it*
> *set with jewels. I was there once*
> *long ago, reached out*
> *to touch a ruby in the wall*
> *pressed my hand over it and wished*

After six months of waiting for buppa she took work
in a cafeteria downtown serving
lunch lines, wore a stiff apron and white shoes, absorbed
shallow language. *Lemon pie, clam chowder*
coffee decaf. Learned to point at the specials board
if her accent was too thick, fill styrofoam bowls
without letting the ladle drip. There are ways
to do the impossible—she learned her place
all over again

On Blackhall street the immigrant wives
watched her come home at six, stared
though the gaps in their kitchen drapes while they stirred
spinach saag, saffron rice
chickpea on the stove. *Aiya, Can you believe it?* they said
Her husband has still not come. Her father
wrote more letters to England, each one sharper
than the last, more full of words for shame. Nights
she wrapped her head with fine bright silk, wore jeweled slippers
that sparkled in the TV light

The Matter Between Animal and Machine Is

Once a hunter killed a goat and watched
the guts come out, saw the concrete cracks
on the floor of his garage grab at the gore
Puddles move, blood running
like children racing out
to the road. Alarmed
the police arrived to intervene
You can't kill a goat, not at home

In India, my father never saw
a plane till he was ten. Imagine
if at birth your eyes were bound with black tape
and then at ten you tore it off and saw:
the enormous lightning beast leaping
through distance, white animal growing
with each blink. "Have you ever heard
a tiger as it kills?" says my father
"It is exactly the sound that a plane
makes when it lands." *We crept into its belly
felt the rumblings as it digested us*

Piara:

> After only a week of Canada
> your grandfather bought a goat
> and slaughtered it in the garage while neighbors
> mowed their lawns

The belly
of the great white tiger hanging over him
skyless

Kurdmyee (I)

The year I turned ten
my auntie Tage hid with my mother in the cloakroom
of the Guru Nanak Temple on Blackhall Street
wearing slippers of the softest silk
Gold tasseling, pale rubies sewn
to her scarlet sari, bangles clanking on her slender wrists
nose and ear connected
by a diamond chain
and *surma* sliding down her wet face

I kept watch for Mahnji at the cloakroom door, balanced
on the piles of big black shoes, camel-hair coats spilling out
into the arched hall
If this will make you miserable
my mother said to Tage, *then you shouldn't*
go through with it

Upstairs in the *Gurdwara,* the holy room
each relative touched forehead to floor
threw hundred dollar bills
into a brass trough at the foot of the altar
covered with wooden lotus

In the cloakroom the sound of Tage's weeping
in the hall noises from the temple kitchen
preparations for a feast—deep pots
full of chickpea, coconut rice
Trays of *jalahbia* and *lardu*
packora and *roti*
being stacked on the counters

I saw Mahnji's red *chuni* first
as she swept around the corner, I
turned fast, lost my footing *She's coming*

My mother and I watched Tage run
to the parking lot, tassels flying
behind her like shining stocks of wheat
her heart beating in our hands

I Tried to Find India in its Poets

I wanted to see a picture of the Punjab
in words, to smell the wood doorsteps
covered with hay
and wild yellow chrysanthemums, the very same
my grandmother threw her wash water on
when she was just a young woman
Souza
Jussawalla
Ramanujan
I tried to find a picture in words

Old stories—Sidhartha, Vishnu, The Black Kali
all dusty statues, huge toes and frozen hair
sandalwood arms
And new stories—Grocery chain stores, airports, catbells and cars
none in between
none that inhabit the space it takes
a yellow flower to grow up around a wood doorstep

I tried to find India in its poets
but I couldn't
they are too busy
finding themselves

I wanted to see a mango tree
in the center of a field, men
melting sugar beneath it, to smell
the cane bake, iron pot flake
the wooden paddles stirring. I looked
for a word that would tell me
the color of shade
the size of a mango tree leaf, and the length
of its shadow at noon. A word
that would show me the black faces of monkeys
paws outstretched gripping a red fruit. What
do I want with airports, catbells and cars?

I tried to find India in its poets
but they are too busy finding Canada
in me

I've never seen her
my grandmother
chrysanthemums the color of lemon rind
around the hem of her dress
tossing the wash water
out of the door
I looked for a Poet to tell me
how she looked then
when her cheeks were smooth like warm sugar syrup
lips red as mangos
how did she look

SORAYA PEERBAYE

My beginnings in theatre-making have significantly influenced my approach to writing. For me, the process is one of investigation through all my senses. I enter the poem's world through skin, through sight, sound and smell, through gesture. I stay attuned to the tension that arises between memory and the present moment, between the experience and its meaning. My experience as a South Asian woman is, in a way, a sixth sense—one that has given me a wider and deeper connection to others, and their sense of being and belonging. It has also given me an awareness of the subtle interplay of difference and power that exists even with those we love, and the choices we make that move us towards compassion and balance. Sometimes, the point of awareness occurs in the experience and is the poem; sometimes the awareness occurs years, even decades later, through the act of writing.

South coast, Mauritius

arc of water rising from the car wheels, translucent ribs
lifting as we plough through rivulets left behind by storm;
in the streets, young men, brown ankles bangled by sunlight
and rainwater. At Gris-Gris, where we walk the basalt shore,
a girl in a green salvar kameez, turned verdant kite
as she runs in salt-arrowed wind; above, seabirds, swept
as Arabic calligraphy. Graffiti by the crumbling stone kiosk
exposing its skeleton of rust at Pointe-aux-Roches
    Ramesh love Primila
        while my small brother, clambering
over tide pools, holds up a starfish, his whole body
starfish as he loses, catches his balance, dances unsteady
      on one foot. But mostly, these
velocity-painted images, as we drive along the coast, me
cyclopean with my eye to the viewfinder: filao trees, fragile
sentinels, overexposed by coral light pouring through late
afternoon, their rows and rows interrupting the slow sun,
frames of film caught in eager machinery, my finger never fast
enough to release the shutter, as I try to photograph
the light, the light   photographs me

The Daughter: Home remedy

Garlic is as good as ten mothers.
—Telugu saying

Spied the first bulb in the living room
as I turned my head from the piano,
imperfect scales, octaves too wide
for my hands. White as a mime's stare,
among all the knick-knacks collected
on the windowsill—seashells, a blown glass
paper weight, some misshapen bowl one of us
made her when we were smaller.

I might have explained it to myself
thinking she'd interrupted her cooking
to open the window. Except
she no longer cooked: spent days
in riddled slumber, nights in
capricious wakefulness, hands now
constantly trembling. When she reached
to comb her fingers through my hair,
I flinched.

The second bulb I found by the shoes
at the front door. I took it back
to the kitchen, not liking
things out of place: its cloves
a cluster of question marks, or so many
eyes, closed, eyelids
fine as vellum, transfused with violet.

Her mother's cookbook keeps a concoction
for cough syrup, made from garlic, fennel, sugar.
When my brother was stung by wasps, it was
crushed garlic we rubbed on his swollen skin.
There are so many uses.
She left bulbs on the balcony, at the edge
of the garage, near the skis and bicycles,
guarding all the entrances to her house,
her self, her family,

from warlocks and werewolves. Their smell
like the garter snake I'd captured late
that summer, secreting acrid milk in fear
and warning. (I threw it away.)

Once, as I pulled my nightgown
over my head, a single
clove fell from the sleeve, cleaved
from the bud. I felt its skin
separate between my fingers: held it,
brittle as the wings of dragonflies, febrile
angels. Her daughter safe, my mother

flew from our house.

Girl, rabbit

I

Fully grown, she seemed bigger than her rabbit smallness. Ears, tail, paws
tucked in, her body spilled and settled beyond her, a white farthingale. Fur
doubled at the chin, an Elizabethan collar: ruffs like lettuce. Ruby eyes glittered,
ambiguous, unchanging in changing light or depth of field. She gazed
imperially over her dominion, towards other continents, seeing neither. She
saw me. My small-mouthed, small-boned determination. She did not trust me.

2

Her name did not fit her: one of those terms of endearment recalling a fair-
weather cumulus. She gnashed her teeth and made *sotto voce,* indignant, piggy
grunts. When I let her out, she caromed across the living room. A thought
jumping synapses. In her cage, she retreated to a corner, glared redly my way.
Thumped. Sneezed, ire peppering her nostrils.

I bargained for her forgiveness with celery hearts and strawberries, though
twice (once to see, and once to show my brother) I fed her a chili. She nursed
scalded taste buds for an hour after. She loved salt from my hand, though
never coming too close—straining to touch her tongue to the crush on my
fingertips.

3

The irrepressible instinct to chew: chair and table legs, telephone wires, the
upright piano, the Oxford English Dictionary, my father's vinyl collection, the
heels of my mother's sandals, my mother's Persian carpet, my mother's cherry
wood standing mirror. The broom bristles left behind when my mother shook
the broom at her.

The instinct to burrow: tear away grass, score the earth, dig. A place where she
was held without hands, sunshine rimming the entrance. Early on she went
further, burrowed past the makeshift fence of picnic chairs. Then my family
and I searched for the comma shape of her, now a white dash in the greenery
of suburbs.

These burrows hurt me. I reached to their centre, felt their promise of home,
their wish for elsewhere. This is how I learned one has to pass through child-
hood to leave it.

4

I bought a leash that I tied to the maple tree, leaving her to nibble blades of grass in summer, root out their frozen shoots in winter.

Once, I heard a wild, high whistling, ran out to the balcony to see her and the neighbour's cat in helical chase, radius of flight tightening with every circuit round the tree. I shooed the cat away, but her screaming continued for several seconds after, breath forced through an unknown organ. As if fear were a syrinx, a muscle reserved for one vowel, one song.

5

The instinct to pull fur. She sat back on her haunches, combed her belly with her front paws, caressed a slight skein into being. It floated as if in wait, the cage glistening strange, amniotic, until strand by strand it came undone and disappeared.

6

I knelt with knees akimbo, so my legs made an M. Nestled her between my thighs. She slipped, hopped from my hold. I planted her back, smoothed her taut ears. She darted. Claws rasped as I grasped her by the haunches. She bit, breaking skin; I squeezed her head down, spanked her across flank. She became still. Fury and fear. Instinct and instruction. I pinned her with one hand, stroked her with the other *love me love me love me* . . .

7

I gave her a stuffed toy as a gift, a pink elephant. She brushed it with her whiskers, nuzzled it, until it tipped over and showed its white rump. Excited, she tapped it, one paw, then the other. Rolled it as though she were making a snowman. Suddenly mounted it, almost falling over as she thrust against it in increasing rhythm. Cage thrummed, a discordant piano. Vegetable pellets added their tambourine rattle. Water in the water bowl puckered, a liquid, quivering nipple. From beneath her the elephant gazed at me, button eyes lumped against its snout each time she humped.

That summer I discovered masturbation, spent an entire Sunday dizzying myself with fantasies of rape and ravishment *I want—I don't care—anything* plummeting under the covers and coming. My mother knocked, I rearranged the pillows and answered weakly. I said I was sick. She put her hand to my forehead, found me feverish, made me stay home from school the next day.

8

Thinking she needed a companion, I bought another: black, with a white stripe on its nose. She made it clear she would not be kindred, pushed the fruit I gave her through the grid into the dung balls below.

I kept them apart, but let them loose together in the living room. He badgered and bragged, tail a flag on hind legs held high. Not quite her size, he pinioned her. Startled her, though she didn't pull away. Their bodies thinned with muscularity and intent. I kneeled to separate them. She fluttered beneath him. He leapt at my hand. Teeth clamped into palm, white electrodes. I stood and raised my arm and he hung on, wriggling in mid-air before letting go.

9

The instinct to pull fur. She combed her belly, loosened the strands. Under the Christmas tree she weaved a nest of tinsel and fur. Sat, fat and content as a creamer.

10

I never saw the kindling.

11

Blind for the first days, the kits were guided by heat. If I held them up to my face, they sought out the moisture of breath. If I stuck out my tongue, they grasped for it, and finding the tip, suckled.

12

They had no scent of their own. She granted them hers: licked their soft bodies, slicked a path to her teats. Let me stroke them.

The day we gave them to the local kindergarten, I brought her blackberries. She nudged them aside, licked my fingers, sniffed the creases of my palm.

13

Sounds in the middle of the night woke me. A metallic clamour. I walked down in the dark. The male reared up on hind legs, gnawed and grunted at the grid. She crouched in her cage, whimpering. A to and fro sound. Rocking. I never saw the kindling. The kits were dead. She rolled one beneath her paws like a rolling pin, its body bruised and slightly bloodied from the pressure of wire and claws. The nest of fur I'd failed to notice already disintegrating.

14

The black one became increasingly territorial, once bulling me so that I jumped onto a chair. I took his cage to the garden, unlatched the door, walked away without looking back. At night, a thunderstorm. Outside, I found a small glistening bundle. Gelatinous from rain. From blood. It reminded me of the colours of licorice. He had wandered into the neighbour's yard: when the cat gave chase, he had run back towards the safety of the cage, but the door swung the wrong way. Stranded, he'd been slashed open, clean as a raincoat.

15

If I lay on my belly in the grass, she would come near and likewise, lay herself low. Eye to eye, nose to nose, we were paper dolls unfolded at the crown.

The doe's instinct to pull fur, as though she could make nestlings as she made a nest. I thought of her making me, beginning with tresses, eyelashes. Hairs raised from gooseflesh. Licking me from head to toe to recognize my scentless body.

As I grew older, she receded from my view, small. At 15, I pushed at the thin stretch of earth between me and sky, adjusted my eyes to the light brimming above. Wild field of adolescence, waiting.

After, taste

"Chai?"

Alchemy of tea   sweet milk
    cardamom

      summoned the triad
          Jahanara
             Saniya and I
        plundering crimson   cigarette packs
          drunk on chai

Harmonium
      intoned the Night Song
          as Jahan resounded

               O girls   let us forget our men
                  flirt   embrace
             make love until dawn!

               (dawn   stubborn
                  long to come   and I crawled
               dumb   into San's bed
               felt her stir   spoon
               her body round mine

                 solemn somnolence

                 sudden absence
              shuddering)

I make chai for myself
take pale pod
    light as beetle carapace
        bite down
      husk splits into wings
          tumbling seeds
      black, mineral

              (bullets
              bullying into body
              body stumbling down)

It's her death I need to crack open
   - the seed of it -

as spoon stirs   stirs
    and pod drops   is caught
       in its slight wake   and
                 released
spun to circumference
     hums perfume   blooms
       green petals

           (rose petals   enclosed
           in mirrored tins
              oxidized to blue
           over years   over years)

Centrifugal force of loss
      Jahan's body in Lahore
    San fled to Brooklyn

In Toronto's east end
    I press stone heat of cup
       between breastbone and palm
   as San's voice sings   through telephone

She teaches me the Urdu word   for story
   Suraiya!   *my ram kahani*   *begs for chai*

       Husked   we do not say her name

Cardamom conjures her

    candied   dark   tingling

      she passes over our tongues

SHARANPAL RUPRAI

In my work I am exploring Sikh religious symbols. The five K's which are the Kesh (uncut hair), Kangha (comb), Kirpan (sword), Kara (steel wrist bangle) and Kachera (loose handsewn underwear) are central as symbols of faith. For many young women and men growing up in Canada, the choice to wear or not to wear these symbols create conflicts with parents, religion, communities, fashion, sexuality and spirituality. While Sikh men are most commonly associated with the wearing of turbans, certain Sikh women have also chosen to wear them. I identify as a Sikh woman and I choose not to wear a turban; however, I have chosen never to cut my hair. I wear a kara on a daily basis, but choose not to wear a kirpan, kangah, or kachera. As a writer, I use the page to figure out my relationship with my spirituality, but also to explore how Sikh women and men are maintaining their religion and culture within a Canadian cultural hegemony.

Kesh

Sacrifice

We used to do this in Kenya
As boys, my three uncles
stand in a line and wait to give mother
yards of wrinkled fabric.
From behind, they look like sisters
their hair down to their waist curls
slightly from being tied up
in a juda.
　　　Grandmother beats
dirt with a long stick, rinses
clean her sons' honour,
and calls for her daughters.
　　　My Mother, with her frizzy hair,
is called in to dry
her brothers' unravelled
turbans in the sun,
in the same way she dries
her chunis. Her youngest sister
holds one end and they wave
the heat of the African afternoon
up and down until they have an ocean
of black between them.
　　　Just as she and I do now in our backyard
for father and brother. My brother
should do his own laundry.
My mother does not tell me if she complained
about being disturbed
from her sidewalk games, or if her sister
cried when her reading was interrupted.
　　　In the morning, the sisters would sit
with chunis on their head
and watch their brothers tie
their turbans before their prayers.

Man of Steel

　　　Father and son stand at opposite ends
of the hallway, with the black starched
material stretched out between
them. The starch creates bumps and waves
in the fabric so my father pulls
one end taut, my brother does the same,
until the sheet becomes a prairie landscape
ready to take seed.
　　　They fold the sheet in half and half again,
an umbilical cord between them.
Bringing himself closer and closer
to his son, my father folds up distance
and leads my brother to the next stage.
　　　In front of the mirror
the student weaves the ribbon around his head
tight and smooth and crafts a small peak at the front
right between his eyes.
　　　Father wears only dress-shirts
and has a jar full of pins
to secure his turban, one in the front
and one in the back. He told us that the pins went straight
through his head and that he was a man
of steel. I knew that my brother would inherit
the jar of pins.

Duty

When Dad died, my brother stood in Ardas
in front of the Guru Granth Sahib
with his head bowed,
my uncle placed blood red cloth on his head.
He was now the man
in the family, the carrier
of the name. Now he needs
my mother or I to stand in
the hallway to help
him stretch out and fold.
My brother's face
softens and I imagine
I can hear my dad's voice
whispering in his ear.
When he fumbles in front
of the mirror, a silence washes over
him and he starts again
the way he was taught.
My brother's hands maneuver
his teachings around his head.
I wonder how it must feel to carry
this weight.

Twins

My father had two tied turbans,
one for work, the other for everyday. The starch
moulded the turban to his head, a helmet.
When I was alone in the house,
I would tie my hair up
in a juda, and put on his turban.
My head held high so the turban would not
tip in front of my eyes, I stood on my toes
to see the boy in the mirror.
　　　A year after my father's death,
my aunt showed me a family photo
of my grandmother, and all her turbaned sons.
My father stood, in the center,
a young me in a turban.
He did not smile with his lips,
but with his eyes.
All the brothers cut their hair
when they went to school in England.
My father, the oldest, grew his hair long again
when his son was born. People tell my brother
how much he looks like his father. A carbon copy.
He smiles with his eyes.

Amputee

A middle-aged Sikh man
walked in without an appointment.
She thought he was very tall
until he unwound his turban
in the middle of the salon.
His mane, thick, clean silk
down to his tailbone, a hairdresser's dream;
he sat down on it and said, *Cut it off.*
She asked him if he was sure.
He nodded and didn't say a word.
      She severed his hair
at the nape of his neck, she would
give it to the cancer society
to have made into wigs. He smiled
and kept his eyes on his eyes in the mirror,
pleased that his sacrifice would help
someone else, a very Sikh thing to do.
He didn't touch his head
when he got up from the chair.
He looked shorter, and didn't tip her,
didn't know it was the custom.
He left and never came back for a trim.
      I look away at clippers, razors
and a fur coat floor. She styles
my hair, parts it on the side, fashions
me a boy and asks *what's it going to be?*
A perm, colour, or cut?

Kachera

To the Rescue

I have something to show you
Always up to something, my Naniji
is sitting half naked on the bed. Her kameez
has embroidered roses against a vanilla weave.
She has yet to put on her salvar.
As a master seamstress at the age of seven
she sews all her own clothes
even her special kachera for travel.
She points at the hem of the
handmade underwear and explains
In here 100 pound, I chuckle
and carry her suitcase to the car.
　　　Naniji can see it all
A thief on the airplane steals
my grandfather's wallet,
but Naniji knows the score
she advised her husband not to worry
she would be back in a flash,
Superhero in action.
In the tiny airplane bathroom
she unties her salvar
and then the nali of her kachera,
she slips out The Queen of England.
Her Majesty with a slight smile
winks at Naniji, two old hens ready for any crime.
With royalty in hand, she glides back to her seat
hands over the money—and thinks
what would he do without me?

Five Day Sin

My mother insists that I wear
homemade underwear. She takes my measurements
and I clinch my pelvis, stomach, thighs and bum cheeks
praying the numbers
would work in my favour. Kachera are too much
like baggy shorts with a draw string.
She buys light blue, tells me it's more
feminine than pure white, the softest
broadcloth she could find
along with nylon nali easy to tie and untie.

She didn't grow up in this country, doesn't know that girls are sizing each
other up and checking out who is wearing a bra or bright coloured underwear,
not the ones that come in a package but the ones where you have to buy each
panty separately.

I covet those panties.

My mother and grandmother
are on a mission from Guru Gobind Singh.
There was no getting out of this one;

I was stuck in time, but my body   body   my body bled for five days.

The menstrual pads did not stick
to the homemade underwear,
and blood trickled down my thigh
I was sent home for stomach pains.
Tampons were out of the question.

They broke down and bought me a package of five oversized-white-no-name-
brand underwear. I was told Guru Gobind Singh would forgive me for wearing
panties for five days out of the month.

Never did I have cramps
or what the boys called p.m.s.
Each month, I willed my body
to release as many eggs
as it wanted, as long as I bled
for five days, so I could be
like the other girls.

3

nine

    fifteen

didn't   know

    he did

i   was   not

    wearing *kachera*

basement bollywood porn

I'm at a party   porn is on in the basement   girls and boys laugh and all I
can think about is the plot of a Sikh porn movie   typical beginning   girl
meets boy with parents   and then the parents disappear into the other living
room and they are left alone to hold hands and almost kiss just like in all the
bollywood movies except   in this script they really do kiss and he touches
her and she smiles and she touches him and then there's music of course
they retreat to the girl's bedroom where clothes come off and there's no sexy
Victoria secret panties here it's all about the nali and being tied up taking out
knots is not easy at the best of times especially when you have to go to the
bathroom sort of the same feeling   so they rip off each others' kachera and
well I am sure you have seen a few and after all when we're naked we pretty
much do it the same way except   so there I am writing the script for my
Sikh porn movie when I am thrown into the closet with what's his name and
it's dark and I can feel fur and then a hand and I yell out a shriek and I bang
into the door and fall face first onto the floor the girls asked what he did and I
shrug my shoulders and they all laughed   and called me a nun

Rootless

In the mirror a 49 year old
woman admires herself in spandex.
For the first time in her life she has taken off
her kachera. She has never been
in a swimming pool, never felt the water
between her legs, never knew
she could be buoyant.
The body has grown accustomed to being planted.
In the pool her legs move like the roots of a red radish,
she kicks and twists in search of ground
and remembers a time when she was confined
she exhales   legs sink still she's weightless, a woman
on the moon. Wide-eyed she dives
head first into the water
observes headless torsos with long limbs
and hears wet dry land noise
of a language she pretends to know.
Her body glistens as she surfaces
wet black hair across her face
her hands on her hips she surveys
the pool like a lifeguard. She dives back in to check
if she could breathe underwater.

Kirpan

1

Joti this is for you one day you will be here standing in front of this poem, you will seek it out like I did this poem will be waiting for you to pick it up and read it out loud again and again and again   this will be your Kirpan and it will keep you alive keep you keep us together   I failed you once didn't know how to help didn't have a voice then   still a voice is not enough in a world full of chanting and watchful eyes   I will not fail again   I promise to write the truth for you on this page so you can make them stop chanting and blink tears away and breathe out scream out this poem

2

It was mace that my brother wanted me to carry or pepper spay for protection in this western city, none available in canada so a Kirpan will have to do he said, a small one to carry by your side just in case those blind dates off of matrimonial sites turned sinful it didn't seem to bug him that the boys might carry one too, he knew that they would be scared off of a strong Sikh girl who would wield a Kirpan in the air and scream at the top of her lungs that was all that was needed a little blood would be enough to scare any boy away   Sikh armour touches my thigh and I take it out of the sheath and use it to butter my bread and stab thick mango slices and place them into my mouth the clean shaven Sikh boy in front of me leaves the table and doesn't come back to pay his half of the bill

3

Dad never used his Kirpan that day in the parking lot that day when the white boys came around at dawn, Dad was getting out of the car getting ready to do his part of the prayers in the Gurdwara they called him a paki and pushed him around two against one he stood right in front of the entrance the gate keeper he was in white head to toe, he must have looked like a ghost to the boys who ran away when they saw the other men behind Dad coming to help those other men asked Dad why he didn't use his Kirpan and he said *they're only boys* and he walked in to wash up before he took his place beside the Guru Granth Sahib

4

only monks could sit on the stage and lead the singing at this Gurdwara in
winnipeg and then it happened   with god in her eyes she took her place on
the stage her husband beside her ready to play the tabla she asks in her princess'
voice to play the vaajai they tell her no and she looks to her sisters and asks
again a lion's roar sweeps through the hall washes over the women   no reply
the monks ask her   to leave and she stands up tall her voice her Kirpan and
asks the women to follow her out with her hands humbled in front of her, her
green chuni on her head, her Kara on her right wrist her Kirpan across her
body she strides out without glancing back   from that day on god became a
Woman and she was in need of warriors

5

never trust anyone as she puts her socks into her overnight bag, *never trust any-
one with the rest of your life* tears drop on my hand and all I want to do is throw
her into a car and take her with me   take her away where no one will find
her too many women I have seen in this place   *never trust anyone not even
your mother or father*
she was packing up her things going back to the mother-and-father-in-law
who threaten her with their Kirpan and a husband who did the same but only
in the bedroom   *never trust anyone who says they're from a good family*

listen she grabs my shoulders my outline in her eyes I know the word that got
her here and she knows the word that will get her out but right now she is
stuck in forever
          never has slipped out the back door she needs to run after it
she rests her Kirpan, a polished mirror into the palm of my left hand she
marches out the door

don't be afraid to use it

SANDEEP SANGHERA

This collection is the result of a number of trips taken to India (in life, in dreams and in books) and in growing up amongst Indian women: storytellers, mythmakers, practicers of the art of the oral tale. Poetry. It is what happens when one is raised amongst women—including a grandmother who could not read nor write—who carried their stories from the "motherland" to Canada, stories of a land loved and left and the complexities and gossip of a "simple" village life. These stories I learned as a child at the knees of these women. Now, they influence my poetry.

An Indian Predicament

every immigrant indian woman
is the bearer
of a staticky phone call

dispatched from the subcontinent
to amrika—can-e-da—in-gland

delivering news
of the mislaid step

a sister's son
a second cousin

drowned in the village well

dirt
stolen in darkness
births into four dirt walls

my grandfather's house

walls

housing sacks of grain
the bread of the gods

in mexico
a random growth of corn is never cut down
and bread
—pan del muerto—
is given to the dead

in my mother's paternal house
a mother stash of chapatis
wait for my grandmother's hands
to be born

wait

until the floods come instead

SANDEEP SANGHERA

flooding the food of gods
out
of a house of stolen walls

that flood taking those walls too

in india, a woman's reputation as a suitable wife is made
(or unmade)
by slapping perfectly round
(not so round)
chapatis onto a skillet

my mother has the reputation of a rani/a queen

mine
stick to the fingers
taste
too much of flour

predict a man-less future

The Women in this Village

the women in this village
are the running off kind

leaving

saucers (not cups)
stained with lip marks
and chai

papers
documenting primary school marks

pundits, charts and prophecies

slates
carrying the awkwardness

of a first son's
meticulously
drawn lines
of the first alphabet

leaving
all that marks the beginning
of a making
of a life

running off

taking

only their babies and their men on their backs

Centavos for the Village Idiot

for one who will not supplicate himself
will not
speak from his knees
for stale bread

centavos

for one village idiot

hidden
on this body that will not beg
will not
ask for a man's touch

centavos

rooted from gutters
fished out of wishing wells

collected
for a beggarly kind of love

Village Witness

i will lead you

into a land
into the shadows of a room

under a delhi sun
we will stand

in a land i was born in
in the lines of a room i was birthed in

in heat

we will stand
on solid ground

in delhi heat

i will tell tales

of the things that happen when ground gives way

monsoon rains stealing
that spot
where life began

(though you still will not believe)

still a village will bear the weight of my tale
and the weight of your disbelief

For An Aunt

my poa-ji died today
her name i have never learned

i know only this

an illiterate woman
who grew her sons into
a pilot
a physicist
a politician

Translation

in mexico suicide is a verb

translated
not into the telling of what has been done
(he committed suicide)

but

translated
into the doing
translating that hand that ended that life

he suicided himself
the mexicans say

Red

never wear red to the wedding of an indian woman

red (in the east)
meaning not lust but luck
and love

red
meaning the colour of the bride

never wear white to the wedding of an indian woman

white (in the east)
meaning the end of life
and living
death and celibacy … celibacy and death

never wear nothing to the wedding of an indian woman

the old widows at the backs of the temple walls
—those dealers in gossip—
will gasp

Indian Logic

my uncle bit on the fruit of his tree
a guava fruit a guava tree

a seed planted itself in the root of his jaw

prophesying the beginning of a lifetime of aching
of weddings and births of grandchildren
of deaths and his own cremation

endured
with that seed paining

he cut down the tree
that bore the most beautiful of fruit

my aunt
spotting a first cavity in the making
had her teeth all removed

now she sits grieving

her sister followed suit

i am the niece of two aunts and an uncle

and the daughter of a woman
who plants a mango seed in Toronto

SHAUNA SINGH BALDWIN

Poems that rise from moments of heightened perception arrive like uninvited guests, brimming with their own imperative, asking my mental re-adjustment as they take up temporary residence. Others have slower beginnings, gradually shifting my perspective into the persona in the miniature realm of the poem. Once the first stirrings and scratchings in my journal appear on screen, I read aloud, examining rhythm, flow and negative space—the spoken implies the unspoken, and each word implies its opposite.

Cruising the Personals

Am in cyberspace, reading acronyms
understandable to initiates
"SWF, DWM, SBF"
with my heart adorning my sleeve.

I beg for someone to steal it,
like some rusty but well-insured car.

If this were my first entry into grihasthashram[1],
my parents would have been online with me,
"inviting correspondence" for a "very attractive,
well-educated, athletic, Indian IT consultant,
born and raised in the UK, blend of East West Culture."
And they would have approved a slim Indian girl
"very beautiful, never married, working as a
vice president, family oriented."
And she'd have long black hair.

But their duty's done and failed,
I'm back on my own a few years later,
"inviting correspondence" from
strangers, preferably Indian.
Who shall I ask for this time?

Another slim girl with long black hair.

I could risk adding to the online ad
that logic flow and algorithms
cannot rescue me, that I need someone
to listen without judgement or payment.
Someone to hold me
in the dark and say, "I see."

[1] Householder stage of life

Gurpurb

What of my festivals?
I have ten.
One for each Guru's birthday.

Close the stores.

No, open them.
Let's shop.
I need your money
and I want things.

My holidays float
past Christmas,
Hanukkah, Easter.

Tell the bakeries:
Learn how to make
parshaad and laddoos.

And tell Hallmark
to start a new line of cards
for Sikh people.

Incorporation

Ghost people ride with me,
Muzzle my outrage, authorize me to share
knowledge or hoard it. Sometimes I am
their spokesperson, and often they
use my body as a billboard
my hands to do their work. Their hunger
steals the knowledge of my ancestors,
patents the seed before it flowers to
basmati, turmeric, and neem.
Bodyless, they grow and brand
themselves on my horizon.

We who believe in non-fictions
have for centuries now
suspended our disbelief
in the legal fiction
that brings them to being.
Now their names are our familiars,
repeated like incantations.
We trust them with our lives
in hospitals, our children in schools.

I tried this at home, once: exposed my soul
to the elements, and the next thing I knew,
a ghost person had incorporated
itself around it. A new entity now
accompanies me everywhere, asking for
minimal intervention, limited liability,
and less oversight.

Memorial

With a few lines on paper
you structure a war memorial,
that will cozy up to a ramp
conveying cars uphill.
And as its architect you explain
the strain of translating abstractions:
Freedom, Democracy, reasons
a nation goes to war,
the difficulty of integrating
high concept with vernacular landscape.

We turn to your screen for a concrete
representation. It obliges with simulation,
a virtual walk-thru of rooms
to be decorated with the weight of memory.
From two dimensions, we mentally create three.
In the fourth lie the Great War, Good War,
Forgotten War, Cold War, Vietnam War,
First Iraq War, Second Iraq War.
And all the little genocides
permitted in between.

You describe a void at the center,
where a strong golden light
will one day break through.
You call it the beam of Liberty.

Lobbyists will gather in the lobby.
Airmen will tell bold tales of bombings.
Seamen will point to battleships and carriers.
Infantry men will enshrine their boots and guns.
We will translate but not transliterate the idioms:
The Proxy War, the Lost War, the Oil War,
The war for the sake of war. Ongoing war.

We'll build this memorial to sacrifice,
ask if this utopia was worth the blood we shed.
We will not mention those who fought
against us or at our side.
Old men ask for recognition, commemoration;
young architects oblige.

"Perhaps Madagascar"[2]

When I reached Germany
I applied for asylum.
"I specialise in fluids,"
I told officials. "In absorbency
and mixture. I aspire to
a life of inquiry
or a life like your own.
That's not a crime here, is it?
It is, where I come from."

"Wait," said the officials.
I wait in a room with a bed
and four other men with the same
scared pall on their faces.

The bathroom is where we go
to be alone when we cannot bear
the screen: angry shouts of protesters,
academics sounding reasonable
about "Turks."
"Ship them somewhere," one suggests.
"Perhaps Madagascar."

I fill a bathtub, step in.
Recall Archimedes,
revise his principle:
an irregular body
displaces a volume
of hate larger than its tangible self,
liquid hate releasing from fear
deep in the molecule.

[2] Suggestion of TV guest discussing migration in Europe on MSNBC.

SHAUNA SINGH BALDWIN

Reincarnation Has No Biblical Basis
—Indianapolis Star

Mr. Billy Graham is very certain
that reincarnation cannot serve me.
He says I can't be rid of my sins
by returning again and again
hoping to live a better life.
That I better put my faith
securely in Christ.

But oh, Mr. Graham, Mr. Graham,
your certainty puffs you into print,
bulbous as a fat balloon. Your certainty
that there are no other gurus worth hearing
struts down newspaper columns,
flows into lead, fires from guns
when helmeted crusaders take to the sky
against the infidel, your blessings on their weapons.

So when your Guru Christ rose
on the third day, is it not possible
—just perhaps!—he was reincarnated,
and even so might fill the hearts of those
not quite as certain?

Return to Wonder

In spring
I return to wonder
as a camel calls upon
water from its hump,

I return to wonder,
carving it
from emaciated air
inducing it—

not from the
rubbing of genie lamps,
the recitation of wishes,
puffs of smoke,
the palming of cards,

but from irises
pushing up in their patch,
bursting through soil,
valiant purple.

I return to wonder,
snatching it
from the press of should-dos
distilling it
from the tug
of schedule and event
to my involuntary present.

Without wonder
I might bear winter
in me always

Then
there might be
nothing to admire

beyond my own being.

So in spring,
I return to wonder.

Shauna Singh Baldwin

The Night She Left Lahore

The night she left Lahore
an unstained moon had
risen over the compound walls,
simplifying the sleepless city
plating dross, grime and rage
to the patina of silver
even as war-cries rolled across
the hot plain. Indians coagulated
into their religions—Hindu, Muslim, Sikh.
A new country spawned
its amoebic shape within the map: Pakistan.
"Hurry up," whispered her husband. "They're coming."
No time to mention
the loveliness of the moon.

She reached for his turbans, stiff with starch
upon the clothesline, folded them
by lantern light. Locked them into trunks.
He loaded the guns, gave one to each
young man he'd mustered. And when
they stood ready, one at each window,
some crowded on the roof, he said,
"Hurry up, will you? They're coming."

She needed to clean the ashes
out of the clay oven. Wanted to sweep
the veranda clean. But she ran to
collect a little money, jewelry,
tied it in a bundle.

In the lane outside, the horse pulled at his
traces, snorting in the "blood-scented dark."
Her husband gave the reins to
their eldest son, helped her in.

She needed to wash her hands,
needed to pray. Perhaps she
should have tucked more
valuables out of sight
wiped the ground a last time,
lovingly, but she remained
breathless in the loaded cart.

"Hurry up," he hissed, as he brought
their little ones. Dream-laden,
their weight moved from his shoulder
to her lap. He flicked the reins
in her son's hands—"Go now,"
he said, "I'll come soon."

So she left, and he stayed.
And the border came down.

More than fifty years later,
she wonders, would they not be
together now, had she lingered
to wash her hands
had she lingered to pray
if she had found some corner
of the veranda to clean again.
From leaden nights on her
charpai in Delhi she lofts her
question across the border
to Lahore: "What shall I do now
with the loveliness of the moon?"

PROMA TAGORE

Proma Tagore finds inspiration for her writing in the multitudinous histories, lives, struggles, movements, and voices of women of colour. Both in her work and in her creative writing, she is interested in themes of immigration, racialization, colonization, community, home, desire, and belonging from a South Asian lesbian perspective. She understands poetry as a deeply intimate and creative site, a place where conversations toward envisioning more just and compassionate worlds might begin.

on a quiet day, i can hear

> *Remember this: We be many and they be few. They need us more than we need them. Another world is not only possible, she is on her way. On a quiet day, I can hear her breathing.*
> —Arundhati Roy, from "Confronting Empire"

on a quiet day, i can hear
the coming and going of footsteps
on newly thawed ground, the sound
of scars shaped like trees and choke-cherry leaves
that mark the way we love and how we've found
ourselves in history.

on a quiet day, i can hear the etchings of new maps,
homes carried on our bodies, our backs,
willed by our own hands, built out of shards
and fragments of re-memory.

on a quiet day, i can hear
the shapes of silence breaking,
stories of our own making,
resilience singing out
in all textures of brown:
earth, mud, clay, bark.

on a quiet day, i can hear her breathing.

accounting for colonial time
for Toni Morrison

it was only a river
that separated the present from past,
that distanced one state from another,
that marked one kind of un-freedom from
something different.
but if someone were to ask
whether that river was big or small,
the river might answer
that its time cannot be measured,
its journey still not over,
and besides,
the past was never distant, and
that river was never only
a river.

it was only a sea
that separated 'us' from 'them'
and distanced one version of history from another,
that re-routed a few hundred years from
something longer.
but if someone were to ask
whether that sea was too big or too small,
the sea might answer
that its memory lies deeper than its waters,
its scars stretch across borders,
a beginning and end never exacted,
bodies never counted,
and besides,
that sea was never only
a sea.

november 14
for Reena Virk

> *I am working out the vocabulary of my silence.*
> —Muriel Rukeyser, "The Speed of Darkness"

in places where knowledge is impossible,
your story lives resilient and gives me new breath,
and your telling shatters the grammar of my silence,
as we begin working out the vocabularies and pathways
of voice.

in remembering,
our rage will hold,
our words will refuse to be kept,
and i will not be consoled
tonight.

when places leave

when the places we are
reside in another land,
when the soil that sustains
is torn by winds, and the waters
on which we travel
see no end,
it is time to discover another way of knowing,
another way of being.

like the chasms of memory,
the gulfs of language,
the rifts of geography,
and the shifting ground
where we may or may not stand,
but inhabit other-wise,
this body speaks
words that are broken,
that are not whole,
but that form a seam,
a juncture that cannot always be seen,
but is felt, constantly,
the way a scar,
long after it is dried up and been (un)forgotten,
feels.

feel me next
to you.
my presence as real and as tangible
as the breath that settles,
the weight that presses,
and know all the places my body has been,
that form the shape and structures of its dreams.

connect bone to tissue to breath,
and let me leave
to a land
I do not know how to be,
and know what I do not yet understand of me,

help me to revisit
all the places that have left me,
all the departures I must take
                    everyday.

missing pieces

ever since,
        i've been holding on so tightly.
trying to hold something larger than my own life,
something buried under the soles of my feet,
in clenched fists, in stomach knots, in locked jaws,
inside, where it is deepest. in the meantime,
grinding teeth wears away, wears down,
makes heavy and tired, want to sleep away,
                yet when I try, my muscle and bones crumble and collapse to
                    fragments of myself, broken.

four when I lost her,
thirty and still grieving,
craving material necessities—

her air to breathe, her red-brown soil
that warms my toes as I burrow,
her soft brown skin to bury inside and under,
her folds of fleshy tummy and breasts,
her roads, her arms that carried and held
just right—

warm scented jasmine night soft moss growing woolly leaf tickling eyebrows
and chin red ants crawling rivers rocking soothing to sleep.

all this time, i've been thinking that i held her,
when she holds me.

when I don't know this,
that's when I grieve.

I will not miss, just always remember
                to leave my door open

for you.

the journey your body speaks

you quest through pieces and fragments
of a story passed on through tongues,
through dreams and channels of vision
made for the sharing.

you walk on cold, watery shores,
through rainclouds sitting heavy
on heart body spirit.

stop holding, let flood—
transform your anger to tears,
knowing I know something
that you were not yet able to speak.

your body is soft and warm
unlike others,
it knows the art of weaving cocoons
for shelter, when nobody else will care,
it knows how to journey to the other side,
how to prepare intelligence out of illness,
how to conjure up a poet's dream,
how to reach higher points of solitude,
it feels from inside.

it knows how to make maps in places that no one else knows how to see.
it knows how to build a road, and find the way home,
guided by remnants of love and friendship alone.

you feel from the inside.

you've tasted your own desire
in the form of a woman's body.
you will travel here again,
from the inside.

like the thirsty long for water

why not just flow,
through deep and heavenly waters, an oceanic reverie.
do not swim, but become the sea, become
smooth silk sand, or carpets of velvet algae,
green and pink and slippery, carpeting solid rock.
whether the teeth of hard crusted barnacles,
overcupped by the tender rubber skin of sea anemones,
sucking me in, undulating, making my ears and spine quiver.
or varieties of seaweed: plump and hollow, a woman's belly;
faded yellow ropes, leaves wide and thick, sheathed in indigo beauty,
wrapped, tangled, entangled in the ocean's mystery.
waves lapping, slapping against skin, against shore, like tongues
swapping stories, song, between each other.
why follow?
why not just flow,
and be grateful for the gift of simply being able to see
things not as they appear, but as they are.

between tongues

lal mati	red earth
poka pakhi	insects birds
akash khola	open skies
alo bhora	the weight of light
rail-garir awaj	the sound of trains
phaguner naram hawa	soft spring winds
pathar madhe katha	the speaking of leaves
gach theke gach galpa	the story of trees
kalpanar daka	through a calling of dreams
chotobalar gantha	childhood weaves
ghumer bhasha	in the language of sleep
phire asha	and returns

painting

time is not a linear thing,
as most of us imagine.
no beginnings and endings,
but multidimensional like you and me.
like the way a moment separates from itself,
then multiplies, existing everywhere,
never lost, but always to be found.

my past lies heavy on you,
transforming your body into an ancient place,
into the magic of my childhood,
into the sorrow of languages lost,
into the labours of many pilgrimages,
a meeting-place,
a palimpsest,
my un-forgetting.

gracious and accepting,
your body bears the weight of my stories,
my trials and my burdens,
yet is not broken, or made heavy by them,
simply holding, containing my inscriptions,
gently, kindly,
for what they are.

making your body foreign
to itself, you teach
that un-knowing
is not a site of loss or betrayal,
but a place of mystery and enchantment,
an invitation to journeys not yet taken,
a turning-ground,
something to trust,
the seams that weave together
the meaning of between.

khichuri after noon

. . . We never did
mention the word, unqualified: I love:
your hair, I love: your feet, toes, tender nibbles: I love:
I love . . .
—Olga Broumas, "Four Beginnings" from *Beginning With O*

speaking strictly,
my hybridized tongue dreams,
all in one breath,
of ginger and cardamom tea,
four o' clock noodles and sauce,
of cumin, coriander, of cherry tomatoes
on the side, a little bit of cake and some ice-cream—

       while,

soft and casual, is how she tells me:

"i love what we do to your kitchen,"
her words in proper time.

avoiding stricture, i know enough to tell,
"oh, i love, too"—
       unqualified.

some notes

1. "on a quiet day, i can hear"

The image of "scars shaped like trees and choke-cherry leaves" is deeply indebted to Toni Morrison's *Beloved*, as is the notion of "rememory."

2. "like the thirsty long for water"

The title is a loose translation of a line from a love song (*baalam avo humre geh reh*) written by the Indian poet, Kabir Das, 1398-1518, where he compares the restlessness of his passion to thirst for water. Kabir wrote in the tradition of the *Bhakti* movement, a popular social and religious movement particularly strong between 800-1700 AD, which argued that divinity could be apprehended solely through devotion or love, and that it was accessible to all people, without restrictions of caste or gender. The *Bhakti* movement has strong affiliations and resemblances to Sufism, Vaishnava Hinduism, and aspects of it have also been incorporated into parts of Sikhism—all of which functioned to challenge elitism in religious traditions. Part of what distinguishes the practice of *Bhakti* from more elite ascetic traditions within Hinduism, for example, has to do with its elevation of and worship of the body, as opposed to the ideal of bodily renunciation that is central to asceticism.

3. "khichuri after noon"

Khichuri, which literally means "jumbled up" in Bengali, is the name of a dish where rice and *dahl* (lentils) are cooked together. I grew up knowing my mom and grandmother never to say the word until it was after the noon hour, because, otherwise, they would tell me, the whole day would be jumbled. As a result, if *khichuri* was being planned to be cooked in the morning for lunch, code-words would have to be found in order to talk about it.

PRISCILA UPPAL

I have always agreed with Aristotle about one thing: while history tells us what happened, poetry tells us what may happen. I don't believe in autobiography. I have never felt the urge "to tell my story"; in fact, I have consistently resisted the notion. Poetry is not about *me* specifically. Poetry is first and foremost about the imagination, and loyalty to the tenets of the imagination (possibility, experimentation, freedom) must exist before any poet can hope to write one meaningful word. While my history can at times offer a starting point for a poem, to document my life does not interest me. My life changes with every word I commit to paper. As a poet and as a human being, I know I have many lives to live and many more to imagine. *Poem for a Runaway Mother* acknowledges and anticipates the many more I have, and will continue, to lose.

Poem for a Runaway Mother

Runaway Mother

I track you in my sleep, a rearview face
Your back a long road sleek with rain.

From town to town it seems you turn
Once a tree, a stop sign, the main exit,

Your hair the last banner to take the curve
And a barrage of dust to stun me.

Underground days, at night I pick up the trail
Wonder what you will change into next:

A lark, a border, a highway motel,
The reckless fawn I just ran over with my heart.

Migrant

You left in November, not like the leaves
But like the birds:
You flew

From the nest built by instinct
A trail of feathers to follow
Like storm clouds, floating.
My arms

The nervous grass, stiff
And unrelenting, charted clear shifts
In pattern, bent towards the wind,
Withstood

The atmosphere. Recent death, blizzard
Warnings, the season's chill: scent
Of absence. While below

The equator water continues to breed,
Trees refuse to age. You make a new home
With all the native birds I had come to
Rely on.

Unlike the Dead

Unlike the dead, your flesh gets thicker.
This year I could spin it like wool
On my lap, your hands embroidered
Into mittens, your remembered back
Tatted into a fine tablecloth.

I could lay you out like a tree trunk
Count the years you've been away
Nail the hard wood to a stand
And watch your distance grow
Steadily as moss.

You plump up in the winter, hibernate
In closets and picture frames, make
A nest in the hollow of the pillows
You once fluffed. Even trees are jealous
Of your survival techniques.

I could carve a tiny family
Out of the timeline of our parting.
I could wrap you up like a large blanket.
I could use your legs for firewood.
By Thanksgiving, I could stuff you,

Feast on this grief, and still have leftovers.

Grave Robbers

Underground we went
The basement littered with your papers.
Your things.

We opened an old wooden chest.
Your body was scarred
And staining the corners.
The smell of mould
Astonished us.

Air thick with dead flowers
I crouched in the shadows, included myself
In the company of ghosts.

It was my brother's hands that excavated.
His lap stocked with red dresses
And cheap costume jewelry,
The dust like lice, crawling
Over his skin.

Dig in, he encouraged.
No harm can be done
To a skeleton.

Mistaken Identity

The last time
I went home to see your husband,

My father,
He greeted me at the white door

And staggered.
A tired man's guilt

Shocked by
A woman's figure and long

Dark hair.
I remembered his voice once

On a cold
Afternoon, telling me *better*

To have been
Left at the altar than after ten

Years, better
To have her run from the church

Than me.
Pauses like wilted flowers

Hanging over
The children that wouldn't be.

The last time
I went home to see your husband

The yellow
Wallpaper shone a bright hope

And over
The scuffed threshold I stood

Both of us
Sobbing for the blushing bride.

Hints My Father Gave Me to Your Whereabouts

The backyard would be the first place to go:
Pick up the scattered seeds of radishes
The broken ribs of autumn's rhododendrons
Skim the shell of the pool until it dries.

With these in your pockets check the cellar
The starved bottles of better anniversaries
The withered boxes of apologetic love letters
Store the finds in a sunny place.

If nothing materializes, raid the laundry
Air out the stained sheets of your childhood
The grey hairs of last year's lint bags.
The washing machine rumbles like her tongue.

I wouldn't bother to travel. Trust me
She lives not in our bedroom, but is not
Far from home. Do not be tricked.
A needle in a haystack is not her style.

Preserve anything resembling a body.

Denial

When asked about his mother
My brother claims her death:

Sometimes to avoid questions
Sometimes because he believes it

Sometimes as a pick-up line
For women who love tragedy.

He wraps you up in white satin
And hundreds of yellow daffodils

Spell your name. He insists
We do the best to honour

Our fading memories: even if
They print in black-and-white

Even if our minds flash on
And off like movement sensors.

Still after the lonely women leave
His bed, there are nights he calls

For advice about funerals:
Who should read a eulogy

And whether or not God ought
To be mentioned in pleasant company.

The procession for your passing
Slips by in every breath.

He insists he has no mother:
Only the one we bury in conversation

Thousands of feet underground.

Disappearing Act

The house may be vacant
Your sleeves without a trace
Of silk scarves or high cards.
And you eluded our sight
Marvelously, like a star in daylight.
Yet still magician, we know your name.

White rabbit, white dove
Black cape, black hat.
All set symbols, all subjects speak
To your second coming.
The art of holding one's breath.

But somewhere
Underneath the wooden planks
Of this house, the ground refuses
To be tricked, will sniff out
Your secret compartment

Drag you out by the hair
In front of a stunned audience
Whisper in your ear:
Abracadabra

A Message to Any Half-Brothers or Sisters I May Have

Sure, I've thought about you. Wondered.
Asked myself a dozen questions, about where
You might live, with whom, the type of climate,
Which countries are stamped on your passports.
Sure, I have.

But don't be surprised if the day comes
When the mail I receive goes
Unanswered, when I refuse to unlatch the door,
Or when I too turn from your well-meant longing
Without a single trace or clue.

Such a dominant gene, you understand,
Must run in our family.

Hide and Seek

I

As the child who has spent too long
In darkness panics, I ran from you.
Searched the smallest places
For shelter. Ones tight as stones
And just as common, where movement
Would seem a trick of the eye.

Hard statue I stood
As you scored the land, befriended
Insect, plant, rain.

The sky became a magnifying glass
And burned me.

II

We began counting. Five addresses,
Three cities, two continents,
You picked out easily
The tracks like badly forged documents.

When I wished to give up
Womanhood prevented me.

The rest you know.

III

Soon a dry darkness will be falling
Below your hand
Where I curled up once.

Your little girl waits patiently,
Almost stubbornly,
In the last place
She knows you will look.

Biographical Notes

HIRO BOGA was born in Bombay and has lived in British Columbia since 1976. She is the author of two books: a best-selling novel, *Shahnaz,* which was published by Oolichan Books in 2000, and by Penguin Books in India in 2002; and a book of poetry, *Love Songs for a Tender God.* Hiro lives with her son on Vancouver Island.

RISHMA DUNLOP was born in India and grew up in Beaconsfield, Quebec. She is the author of several books of poetry including *The Body of My Garden* (2002), *Reading Like a Girl* (2004) and the forthcoming *Naramata Road.* She was a finalist for the CBC/Saturday Night Canada Council Award for Poetry in 1998 and recipient of The Emily Dickinson Award in 2003. She is a professor of Literary Studies in the Faculty of Education and the School of Women's Studies at York University in Toronto.

KULDIP GILL was born in Punjab, India, raised in the Fraser Valley, and lives in Vancouver, B.C. with her husband. She received her PhD (Anthropology) from the University of British Columbia and now holds an MFA in Theatre, Film and Creative Writing (UBC). Her recent books are *Dharma Rasa,* (Nightwood Editions, 1999); two limited edition small books: *Cornelian, Turquoise and Gold,* (Colophon Books, 2003), and *Ghazals: Rai and Sohni,* (Frog Hollow Press, 2003).

SONNET L'ABBÉ was born in Toronto but spent her school years in Calgary, rural Manitoba, and Kitchener-Waterloo. Her cultural background can be summed up as half-Guyanese, half-Franco-Ontarienne, but even her Guyanese identity is mixed-up, or "Heinz 57," as her mom called it. She holds a BFA in Film and Video from York University and an MA in English from the University of Guelph. Her first book of poetry was *A Strange Relief* (2001); selections in *Red Silk* are from a book in progress, tentatively titled *Da Da Da.*

DANIELLE LAGAH was born in Victoria, British Columbia in 1977. Her work has been featured in literary journals, on CBC radio, in short film, and in the book-length publications *Breaking the Surface* and *Islands West: Stories from the Coast.* She currently resides on Vancouver Island.

SORAYA PEERBAYE came to writing through the theatre. Her solo performance *GirlWrecked* was produced in Toronto and presented at the ArtWallah Festival in Los Angeles. Her belief in art as a means of human healing has led to her creative associations with Nightwood Theatre, the Desh Pardesh Festival and Conference, and the Canada Council for the Arts, where she was equity coordinator. Currently a grants officer at the Toronto Arts Council, she is also an independent translator and playwright in residence at Theatre Direct. She lives with her husband in Toronto.

SHARANPAL RUPRAI grew up in Winnipeg, Manitoba and is a graduate of the University of Winnipeg. She has taught middle years for three years in Winnipeg. Currently, she is working on her Masters in English at the University of Calgary with a focus on South Asian writing. Her work has appeared in *Exposed,* an anthology of five Winnipeg women writers and *Prairie Fire's* special issue entitled *Race Poetry Eh?*

Born in India, SANDEEP SANGHERA immigrated to Canada in 1975. She holds an MA in English from the University of Toronto and currently resides in Mexico City where she teaches political poetry at a preparatory college. Her literary interests include writings from Latin America, the Caribbean, and the Indian sub-continent. She is at work on her first novel exploring the echoes between Indian classical dance and flamenco, an echo that is used to explore the blurring and layering of cultural identities.

SHAUNA SINGH BALDWIN is a Canadian-American writer of Indian origin. Her books of fiction include the award-winning *What the Body Remembers,* (Doubleday, Knopf Canada, 1999) and *English Lessons and Other Stories* (Goose Lane Canada, 1996). Her new novel, *The Tiger Claw* (Knopf, 2004), has been shortlisted for the Giller Prize.

Born in Calcutta, India, PROMA TAGORE immigrated to Canada along with her family in 1976 at the age of four. She grew up in the small town of Dauphin, Manitoba. She earned her PhD degree in Literature from McGill University in 2000. Proma now lives in Victoria, British Columbia, and has been teaching at the University of Victoria for the past five years in the fields of feminist, anti-colonial, and queer studies. She is currently working on revising her dissertation into a book, which is entitled *The Shapes of Silence: Women's Writing as Testimony.*

PRISCILA UPPAL was born in Ottawa in 1974 and currently lives in Toronto. She has published four collections of poetry: *How to Draw Blood From a Stone* (1998), *Confessions of a Fertility Expert* (1999), *Pretending to Die* (2001), and *Live Coverage* (2003); all with Exile Editions. Her first novel, *The Divine Economy of Salvation* (2002), was published to international acclaim by Doubleday Canada, Algonquin Books of Chapel Hill US, and translated into Dutch and Greek. She is a professor of Humanities and Coordinator of the Creative Writing Program at York University.

.